D1560585

THE
(WHAT TO DO WHILE YOU'RE HOLDING THE)
PHONE
BOOK

THE
(WHAT TO DO WHILE YOU'RE HOLDING THE)
PHONE
BOOK

by
GARY OWENS

illustrated by
CHRIS JENKYNS

Published by J. P. Tarcher, Inc., Los Angeles

Distributed by Hawthorn Books, Inc., New York

No more dedications, please, our time is up.

Copyright © 1973 by Gary Owens

All rights reserved.

Library of Congress Catalog Card Number: 73-83280
ISBN: 0-87477-015-7

Illustrated by Chris Jenkyns
Designed by Cal Schenkel

Published by J. P. Tarcher, Inc.
9110 Sunset Blvd., Los Angeles, California 90069

Printed in the United States of America.

Published simultaneously in Canada by
Prentice-Hall of Canada, Ltd.
1870 Birchmont Road, Scarborough, Ontario

1 2 3 4 5 6 7 8 9

SOMEWHAT FOREWORD

This handy book on telephones was prepared for you by radio and television's beloved Gary Owens, because he has, for a long while, felt many of you were hopelessly screwed up and needed a handy thing to carry--something that could be whipped out when you are confused about telephones, or tired, or suffering from irregularity.

You can use this handy book of information and wisdom just like the Chinese use the thoughts of Mao Tse Tung.

Say, for instance, an obscene caller is bothering you and you want to come up with just the right thing to say. You simply flip to page 59, and _voila_, there it is. (If you'd like to know exactly what to say when someone says _voila_, you'll have to look elsewhere.)

Or say you've just been gored by a live moose in the lobby of the Denver Hilton, and you need to phone the Pope. You could easily check page 21 containing the phone numbers of _really_ important personages and dial direct! (Be careful not to misdial, because one of our readers, upon not checking his dialing finger, read a few soothing pages of this book to the admissions clerk at Mary Baker Eddy Memorial Hospital and great angst ensued.)

So many folks have asked, "Gary Owens, was this handsomely produced, professionally crafted, heartlifting little volume properly tested before publication?" And we answer with a resounding "Finork!!" The same meticulous, careful testing went into this telephone companion book that went into our national nuclear experiments. More than 100,000 copies were buried in the sands of Yucca Flats, Nevada. How's that for concern for you, the pigeon with the $3.95?

Without ever reading the Gary Owens <u>Phone</u> <u>Book</u> you are doubtless already saying to yourself, "My, oh my, I must pass this splendid little tome on to all my friends and relatives after I'm through enjoying it!"

Don't!

Keep it . . . or once you've read it, destroy it! By <u>giving</u> it to anyone you hurt Mr. Owens' chances to make enough money to have his teeth fixed. (He chases cars and recently suffered a nasty dental encounter with some Packard spokes.) Also, he needs to save enough money to pay for the sound thrashing of NBC's Rowan and Martin, and to renovate his all-night shoe repair stand in Burbank.

Tell your friends you like the book, then destroy it right there in front of them. In the event that you don't like the book, keep your mouth shut. We have ways of finding out who you are!

If you don't like it you could send us a lot of money and return the book, and then we will recycle it--probably into something on a roll.

And now, for your first truly great adventure, turn to the first chapter in your new phone book and memorize it.

Jeremy Tarcher, publisher of this book and a man with whom the word "keck" is truly synonymous, has committed each of the pages to memory . . . and shortly we will have Jeremy committed.

I know many of you have had personal battles over your phone bills, and some of you have even questioned the monopoly of AT&T (they usually get Boardwalk and Park Place), and you would like to know more about these pressing problems. I know many of you have wondered if your phone was tapped, and just how to do a magic trick over the wires with a friend. And I know many, many of you out there have wondered where the busiest phone booth in the world is . . .

It's all inside.

Thank you, and thank you F.M.

Harlow Goobley

Earl C. Festoon, Vice-President,
The Gary Owens Corporation

The beat of a different eardrum

On June 2, 1875, a hot, sultry day in Boston, Alexander Graham Bell and his assistant, Thomas Watson, were busy tuning transmitters in rooms about 60 feet apart. Then, by accident, Bell found the clue to electrical speech. Watson had been adjusting the coils of his transmitter when one of the springs had become jammed. As he tried to free it, Bell heard a sound over his receiver in the other room. For the first time the tones and overtones of sound had been transmitted electrically.

By evening of the following day, June 3, Watson had a working model of the first receiver—nothing more than a magnet wound with copper wire and affixed to a thin diaphragm of iron, which served much the same purpose as the human eardrum. Running a battery current through the wire caused a magnetic field to be set up, and when sound waves hit the diaphragm, disturbing the magnetic field, speech was transformed into electrical impulses.

Bell made a few small adjustments to the transmitter, shouting and singing into it as he did so. Soon Watson came running into the room, yelling, "I could hear you! I could hear your voice! I could almost make out what you said!"

I thought you wanted me to stay on the other phone

On March 10, 1876, at Number 5, Exeter Place, Boston, Bell and his assistant, Watson, were trying out the first really sophisticated version of their telephone. Sitting at the receiver, Watson heard Bell's voice shout from the apparatus, "Watson, come here, I want you!" These words have become immortal, for they were the first ever heard distinctly over a telephone—all because Bell had upset a beaker of sulphuric acid on his clothes.

Drunk: Operator, I'd like to phone my wife in Chicago.
Operator: Number please?
Drunk: She's my second one.

Your telephone: electronic ventriloquist

Did you ever wonder exactly what happens when you lift the receiver and dial a number? Well, here's a somewhat inexact version:

Like the light bulb, the phone operates as part of an electrical circuit. The power source is located in the phone company's central office, from which the conductors, wires, and cables lead to the subscriber's phone. When the receiver is lifted the two buttons on the cradle close the circuit and bring you a dial tone that signals "ready

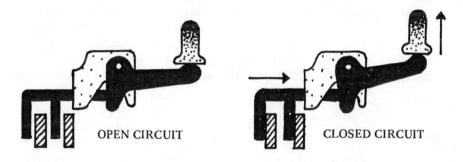

OPEN CIRCUIT   CLOSED CIRCUIT

for calling." When you dial a number, you open and close switches behind the dial that send electrical impulses into the central office switching equipment. (Touch-Tone phones send a pair of musical tones for each number to trigger these switches.)

The first three numbers you dial set up the circuit to the central office that handles the phone you're calling; the last four numbers put you through to the phone itself. If you're calling long distance, the additional three digits, or area code, determine the part of the country in which the central exchange is located. Electromagnets and switch contacts in combination form relays, about seven for every line in use. These relays are activated by each digit dialed, repeating the pulses of the numbers. In this way, the first three digits complete the circuit between your phone and the exchange you're dialing, and the last four digits close the relays that connect you to the single phone you want.

When you speak into the transmitter, the vibrations of your voice are converted into electrical waves. First, the sound waves hit a diaphragm, a circular piece of very thin aluminum, which vibrates against a chamber filled with hundreds of grains of carbon (made from anthracite coal). The movement of the carbon grains is what produces the electrical waves. Each change in sound pressure produced by your voice moves the diaphragm back and forth, increasing or decreasing the amount of space between the carbon grains. Each movement produces a corresponding increase or decrease in the electric current passing through the carbon chamber—more space between grains allows less current to flow; less space allows more.

The electrical impulses from the transmitter then go through the phone lines to your party's receiver, which has exactly the opposite function from that of the mouthpiece: the receiver converts the electrical impulses back into sound waves. It, too, has a diaphragm of

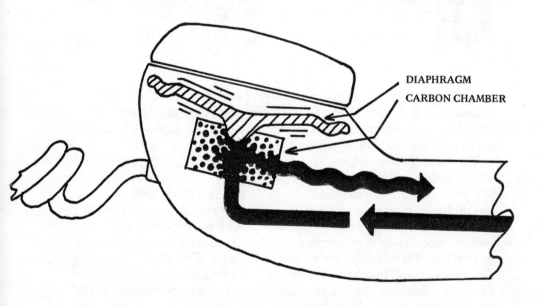

DIAPHRAGM

CARBON CHAMBER

TRANSMITTER

aluminum, with an outer ring of magnetic iron. Beneath this is an electromagnet, a ring of soft metal with a coil of wire around it. Surrounding the diaphragm and the electromagnet is a permanent magnet, providing a steady pull on the outer ring. The varying currents produced by your voice cause the electromagnet to pull strongly or weakly, which in turn causes the receiver's diaphragm to vibrate. By vibrating, the diaphragm imitates your voice.

When you call your party, the bell in his phone receives electric current, causing it to ring. If he picks up his receiver, he completes the circuit to your phone, and the two of you can talk. The voices you hear, however, are not really your own voices. They are reproductions of your voices, reconstructions of their tones and personalities. When you hang up, all of the operated relays and switches release, freeing the lines for more calls.

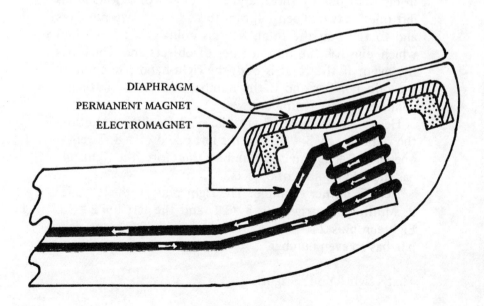

DIAPHRAGM
PERMANENT MAGNET
ELECTROMAGNET

RECEIVER

THE SURE BET

Bet your telephone friend that, if he makes two piles of objects on his desk, one containing an even number of objects and the other an odd number, you can tell him which pile is the odd and which is the even.

After he has made the two piles, have him put one on the right and one on the left without telling you which pile is where. Now ask him to multiply the number of objects in his right pile by three, and the number of objects in his left pile by two. Then tell him to add these two numbers and to tell you the total. At this point you can tell him which pile has the odd number of objects and which has the even. If the total is odd, the right-hand pile contains the odd number and if the number is even the left-hand contains the even number.

Here's an example: Right pile: 7, left pile: 4. Multiply the right pile by 3 = 21, and the left pile by 2 = 8. Twenty-one plus 8 = 29, an odd number; therefore, the right pile has the odd number of objects.

Here's another example: The right pile: 8, the left pile: 9. Multiply the right by 3 = 24, and the left by 2 = 18. Eighteen plus 24 = 42, an even number; therefore the right pile has an even number.

That's right! You're right!

No initial problems

If you have a lengthy name, perhaps running to several words, and you want all of it listed in the directory, the phone company will, if you insist, print it in its entirety. They may grumble about it, but they'll do it.

What's in a name?

The Altoona, Pennsylvania, telephone directory for 1951 carried the longest single-party listing in the history of the Bell System: Wolfeschlegelsteinhausenbergerdorff, Herbert B.

With address and phone number, the listing took up three lines.

Wide-angle name

The longest individual listing in the history of the Manhattan phone book belongs to a press photographer: Hatziconstantinou, Constantine.

If you've got it, keep it

AT&T, the world's largest corporation, lists assets of more than $38 billion. Over three million Americans own its stock, making it the most widely held company in the country by a wide margin. Although the annual sales of General Motors average about $20 billion, compared to $14 billion for AT&T, AT&T's assets are greater than those of GM, Ford, Chrysler, General Electric, and IBM combined.

Sizing up the phone company

Just how big is AT&T? Well, it has complete or partial ownership and complete control of the following operating companies:

New England Telephone & Telegraph (71.4%)
The Southern New England Telephone Company (17.5%)
New York Telephone Company (100%)
New Jersey Bell Telephone Company (100%)
The Bell Telephone Company of Pennsylvania (100%)
The Diamond State Telephone Company (100%)
The Chesapeake & Potomac Telephone Company (D.C.) (100%)
The Chesapeake & Potomac Telephone Company of Maryland (100%)
The Chesapeake & Potomac Telephone Company of Virginia (100%)
The Chesapeake & Potomac Telephone Company of West Virginia (100%)
Southern Bell Telephone & Telegraph Company (100%)
South Central Bell Telephone Company (100%)
The Ohio Bell Telephone Company (100%)
Cincinnati Bell, Inc. (26%)
Michigan Bell Telephone Company (100%)
Indiana Bell Telephone Company, Inc. (100%)

Wisconsin Telephone Company (100%)
Illinois Bell Telephone Company (99.3%)
Northwestern Bell Telephone Company (100%)
Southwestern Bell Telephone Company (100%)
The Mountain States Telephone & Telegraph Company (86.8%)
Pacific Northwest Bell Telephone Company (86.8%)
The Pacific Telephone & Telegraph Company (89.7%), including Bell Telephone Company of Nevada
Bell Canada (2%)
Western Electric Company (100%)
Bell Laboratories (50%—the other 50% is owned by Western Electric, a wholly-owned subsidiary of the Bell System)

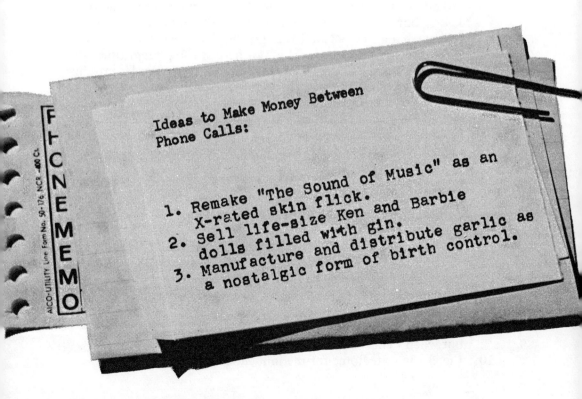

PHONE MEMO
AICO-UTILITY Line Form No. 50-176, NCR .400 Ct.

Ideas to Make Money Between Phone Calls:

1. Remake "The Sound of Music" as an X-rated skin flick.
2. Sell life-size Ken and Barbie dolls filled with gin.
3. Manufacture and distribute garlic as a nostalgic form of birth control.

Smart answering on your device

As for your response on the telephone answering service device, it is important to remember that it should always sound profound and important . . . because you never know what exalted personage may be calling your number.

Here's a Gary Owens handy list of things to record on your answer-type phone.

1. Hello. This is_____. I'm not at home right now. I've been hired as the resident Molester at the Bijou Theater. I'll be back at_____ so, when you hear the beep, give me your name and phone number.

2. Hello. This is_____. I'm not here right now because I'm attending a funeral. Unfortunately, it's mine. I'm dead you know, but, if you would like to leave obsequies and messages telling what a fine person I was, go ahead at the beep.

3. Hello. This is_____. I'm not here at the present time. My dog is answering all calls for me. I sewed a tape recorder into his head and your message will be taken down. I will phone you back when I return. At the bark, give the information (Bark).

4. Hello. This is_____. I'm not here right now because I'm attending the axe murderers convention in_____. Be careful when you talk, as you might get cut off. (Laugh or snicker at this point.)

5. (Use Oriental voice) Hello. This is KATO, Mr. or Ms._____ faithful valet. (He or she) is not in now, but is out solving crimes. If you would like to leave your name, go ahead at the beep.

6. I'm taking my elderly grandmother, who's named me in her will, out for her first parachute jump.

7. I'm out giving a hickey to the Statue of Liberty.

8. I'm out getting anti-freeze for my waterbed.

9. I'm not answering the phone because I feel despondent. The zoo in my hometown had to close down because the duck died, but when I cheer up, I will return your call.

10. I'm at the state home for the innocuous getting a checkup.

WHY IS IT THAT THE WRONG NUMBER IS NEVER BUSY?

Voice telephoning: Is my wife home?
Dummy maid: Who?
Voice: My wife! Is my wife home?
Maid: Naw...who should I say called?

* * *

Secretary: Sir, I think you're wanted on the phone.
Boss: You think! What's the good of thinking?
Secretary: Well, sir, the voice said, "Hello, is that you, you old idiot?"

* * *

Dumb Starlet: Hello, Foonman Dairy? Would you send over a couple
   of cases of milk — I'd like to take a milk bath.
Dairy: Okay. Pasteurized?
Dumb Starlet: No, just up to my chest.

Nikita who? (a true story!)

Just before Khrushchev was overthrown, he went on a vacation. While he was away, his colleagues ordered the phone numbers of all the top Soviet officials changed, and instructed operators not to give out the new numbers. When the coup was launched, Khrushchev was prevented from calling his comrades to enlist their support.

Some numbers to dial when you're feeling important:

NAMES AND ADDRESSES	TELEPHONE
Paul VI (Vatican City)	69-82
Queen Elizabeth II 930-4832 (London)	
Golda Meir -(Jerusalem)	3-92-31
RICHARD M. NIXON 202-456-1414 (White House)	
Aristotle Onassis - 212 PL 3-4500 (St. Regis)	
212-TE 8-8000 (Pierre Hotel, N.Y.)	
Publisher -New York times	(212) 556-1234
General Motors (Hq)	313 556-5151
Miami Dolphins 305-379-1851	
Mickey Mouse: 213 849-3411 (Disney Studios)	
A Swiss Bank (Union Bank of Switzerland, Zurich)	
051/29 44 11	
Wrest Point Casino, Hobart, Tasmania	
SCOTLAND YARD: 230-1212	250-112
New York Stock Exchange	212-623-300
Royal Hong Kong Golf Club	H-92273
Leonid Brezhnev, Kremlin: unlisted *	
HOWARD HUGHES - dial Operator	

*To be expected—all Russian numbers are unlisted,
there being no telephone books in Russia.

LONG DISTANCE AGE AND CHANGE PREDICTIONS

Tell a phone friend that you can guess both his age and the amount of change (less than a dollar) he has in his pocket.

Have your friend write his age on a piece of paper, multiply it by two, add five, multiply by 50, subtract 365, add his change, and tell you the final answer. To this total you secretly add 115 and, if all has been done correctly, the two left-hand figures will reveal his age and the two right-hand figures the amount of his change.

For example:

Friend writes his age		24
Multiplies it by two	(2 x 24) =	48
Adds five	(48 + 5) =	53
Multiplies by 50	(53 x 50) =	2650
Subtracts 365	(2650 - 365) =	2285
Adds change of, say, 56¢	(2285 + 56) =	2341
He tells you a total of		2341
Now you secretly add 115	(2341 + 115) =	2456

The coffee's good, though

By general consensus, the worst telephone system in the Western Hemisphere belongs to Brazil. For a start, there is a long waiting list just to have a telephone installed. One doctor in Rio, on the priority list, waited six years for his. Indeed, the only sure way to get service is to pay a friend $100 or so plus a monthly fee for the right to put an extension on his phone. Or you can buy a phone on the black market for about $700 to $1,000.

Once you have your phone, your troubles are just beginning. Even in Rio, exchanges are disastrously overloaded, and many businessmen employ "noise boys" to do nothing but sit around all day with phones to their ears ready to signal when a dial tone is heard. And in the afternoons, when Brazilians are jamming the lines, phoning their bookies for lottery information, the only feasible form of communication is by messenger.

To get a really accurate idea of the importance Brazilians attach to their telephone system, you have to go back to February, 1966. It was almost Carnival time and, when workers were putting up decorations for the festivities, they severed Rio's major downtown telephone cable. Nonetheless, since repairs would have interfered with the decorating schedule, service was not restored until after the Carnival was over, many days later.

Pay-less phones

Here are a few tips on how you can cut down on your telephone costs:

Always check your monthly bill carefully. If there are any long-distance calls or MMU (Multiple Message Unit) calls you don't remember having made, it's possible that you *didn't* make them. Call the phone company's business office and they can tell you the names of the parties at the numbers listed on your bill. If you have no knowledge of any calls to these people, you can ask that the charges be removed from your bill.

By reporting static and interference on long-distance calls, you can qualify for a credit adjustment based on your estimated degree of satisfaction with the service you received.

When you have to ask an operator to put through a long-distance call, which for some reason you cannot dial direct, be sure to ask for the direct-dial rate—and then check your bill to see that you got it.

If you have asked for any equipment to be removed, examine your bill to make sure that the charges for it have also been removed. Most "extra" equipment involves an additional monthly charge, but some subscribers have gone on paying for such equipment even after requesting its removal.

There are ways of reducing your monthly service charge itself. In some areas, party lines are still available, and—if you don't mind the sacrifice in privacy—they cost about $1.50 a month less than private lines, a saving of $18 a year. Also, there are "Limited Call Options" (also known as "Measured Service") by which you can qualify for a lower rate if you make fewer than, say, 60 calls a month. This will save you about $1.50 each month, or even more if you get the very lowest Measured Service (20 calls a month in most places).

Finally, remember the economy rules for long-distance calls. Dial direct whenever possible. If you can't dial direct, at least try to call station-to-station rather than person-to-person. Try to make all long-distance calls within the "low rate" hours. The lowest rate is for calls between 11 p.m. and 8 a.m., but those placed between 6 p.m. and 11 p.m. cost only 20-25 cents more for the first three minutes. And, of course, be brief. Although you save nothing by talking *less* than three minutes, you do save by not talking *more*.

Things to say to get rid of persistent salesmen

1. Hello, I apologize for answering the phone because I just found out leprosy can be transmitted through the wires . . . the doctor told me my scholastic average just fell off.
2. Hello . . . hello . . . hello . . . I can't seem to hear you hello . . . hello . . . (Then you cleverly hang up.)
3. Hello . . . Say, I'm glad you phoned. I was just practicing my dramatic recitation of "Thanatopsis." I haven't had a chance to do it for anyone yet. Listen to this . . . (Then you recite into the phone.)
4. Hello? (Switch on a prerecorded gunfight and brawl in background with dogs barking.)

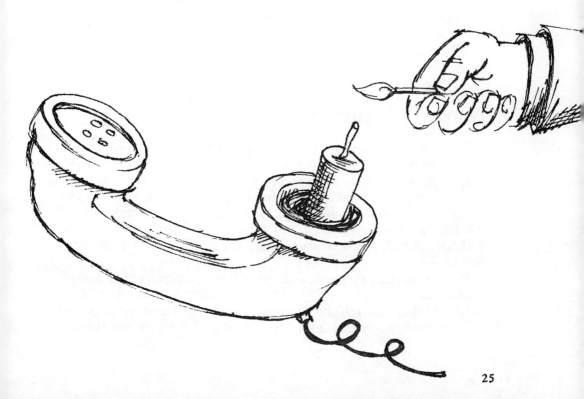

A. G. Bell's "Centennial" Model of 1876.

A measly beginning

Telephone numbers were first used in 1879. Before then, people dialed Central and asked for a party by name. But in that year, during an outbreak of measles in Lowell, Mass., Dr. Moses Greeley Parker feared that Lowell's four phone operators might succumb and bring about a paralysis of service. He therefore recommended use of numbers for calling Lowell's 200 subscribers. Substitute operators, Parker reasoned, could be more easily trained in case of such emergencies.

Bell's historians claim that the telephone management at Lowell feared that the public would take the assignment of numbers as an indignity, but the telephone users saw the practical value of the change immediately and it went into effect with no stir whatsoever.

All they wanted was to talk to themselves

In July, 1879, one of the world's first private switchboards was installed in Columbus, Ohio—at the Columbus Asylum for the Insane. It handled 42 telephones. For some reason, however, the switchboard was not connected to the city exchange until September, 1880.

Where to find a phone

As of January, 1972, there were 291 million telephones in the world. Here's where most of them are:

United States	125,142,000
Japan	29,827,936
United Kingdom	16,143,102
West Germany	15,245,686
USSR	11,980,000
Italy	10,321,581
Canada	10,290,305
France	9,546,173
Spain	5,129,501
Sweden	4,679,691

Other countries with more than a million phones are Argentina, Australia, Austria, Belgium, Brazil, Colombia, Czechoslovakia, Denmark, Finland, East Germany, Greece, India, Mexico, The Netherlands, New Zealand, Norway, Poland, South Africa, and Switzerland.

Presidential telephone quiz

Below is a list of American presidents, followed by a list of curious facts concerning their use of (or disdain for) the telephone. Fill in the blanks with the appropriate letter from the second list. The answers appear at the bottom of the next page.

1. —— Rutherford B. Hayes
2. —— James A. Garfield
3. —— Grover Cleveland and Benjamin Harrison
4. —— William McKinley
5. —— Theodore Roosevelt
6. —— William H. Taft
7. —— Woodrow Wilson
8. —— Warren G. Harding
9. —— Calvin Coolidge
10. —— Herbert Hoover
11. —— Franklin D. Roosevelt
12. —— Dwight D. Eisenhower
13. —— John F. Kennedy
14. —— Lyndon B. Johnson
15. —— Richard M. Nixon

A. Seldom used the phone because of temperament, but allowed one set in the White House for use by the servants.

B. Loved the phone and made daily long-distance calls to his family and friends in Cincinnati when away on affairs of state.

C. Had the first *private line* in the White House.

D. Instructed White House operators *never* to ring him.

E. Was the first President to have a phone *on his desk.*

F. Was the first President to have a phone *in his home.*

G. Was the first President to have a hot line to *Moscow.*

H. Was suspected of tapping the lines of his opponents' party headquarters.

I. Was the first President to use the Trimline Touch-Tone phone.

J. Had an unlisted number for his apartment in Manhattan and was given to forgetting how to dial the First Lady there.

K. Loved the phone and listened to election returns from his home in Canton, Ohio.

L. Disliked the phone and used it only in case of emergency, such as during the Portsmouth Conference crisis.

M. Addressed Congress in 1923—and radio stations in Providence, New York, Washington, St. Louis, Kansas City, and Dallas broadcast the statement via telephone lines.

N. When inaugurated in 1921, spoke to a crowd of 125,000 over a public address system developed by Bell.

O. Had a black and gold "business" phone on his desk.

Answers to Presidential Telephone Quiz: 1-C; 2-F (Garfield's home phone was installed free while he was still a member of Congress); 3-A; 4-K; 5-L; 6-B; 7-D; 8-N; 9-M; 10-E (up to this time, 1929, presidents talked from a booth just outside the executive office); 11-J; 12-O; 13-G (although Eisenhower had hot lines to England and France); 14-I (a *gold* Trimline Touch-Tone, to commemorate installation of the hundred-millionth phone in the U.S. Eisenhower had received the fifty-millionth phone in 1953, just 14 years earlier); 15-H.

29

THE PICK-A-WORD TRICK

If you have a copy of a book or magazine that your phone friend also has, you can "guess" with 100% accuracy any of a couple of thousand words that he picks out of his book.

Ask your friend to open his book to any page he wants and to select any word in the *first nine lines* and *within nine words of the left margin.* Then have him multiply the number of the *page* by ten, add the number of the *line,* add 25, multiply the sum by ten, and add the number of the *word* in the line.

Now ask your friend to give you the result. Suppose he says 11,704. Secretly you subtract 250 from this number, leaving 11,454. Divide that total like this—114-5-4—and you know that your friend has picked *page* 114, the fifth *line* and the fourth *word!* Just look up the word in your edition of the book and tell him what it is.

Example: If your friend picks the 26th page, ninth line and fourth word, he would multiply the page number by ten (10 x 26 = 260), add the number of the line (260 + 9 = 269), add 25 (269 + 25 = 294), multiply the sum by ten (294 x 10 = 2940), add the number of the word in the line (2940 + 4 = 2944), and give you the result. Then you would subtract 250 (2944 - 250 = 2694), and divide up the total in the following manner—26-9-4. Now you know that your friend's page number is 26, his line is the ninth, and the word he chose is the fourth.

Things to do
while waiting for the phone to ring

1. Shave your head . . . then with a felt-tip pen draw on a current hair style.
2. Have your teeth pulled.
3. Learn to play the zither.
4. Sew your uncle's nostrils together while he's sleeping.
5. Develop a re-cycling device for fried mush.
6. Glue chicken feathers to your body.
7. Learn to speak 15th-Century Portuguese.
8. Go from room to room on a motorcycle.
9. Develop a hobby of collecting dead beavers.
10. Pray to Pat Buttram as a religious idol.
11. Carve a replica of Mount Rushmore out of soap but, instead of Washington, Lincoln, Jefferson, and Teddy Roosevelt, use Ginny Simms, Tab Hunter, Sandra Dee, and Hugh O'Brian.

(More things to do while waiting for the etc.)

12. See if you can run around Orson Welles in under one minute.
13. Think of ways to avoid getting whooping cough and lockjaw at the same time.
14. Knit a whoopie cushion with only bailing twine and small amounts of whoopie.
15. Take pictures of your varicose veins and sell them to Rand McNally as roadmaps of Arkansas.
16. Cut out toy zeppelins from your flocked wallpaper.
17. Practice your Katherine Kuhlman imitations.
18. Train your 2,000 pet bees to spell out an obscenity by stinging the seat of a fat neighbor.
19. Tie your shoes — or beat them in an overtime.
20. Bring several parking meters indoors . . . and watch them violate themselves.
21. Get a picture of Doris Day, Arthur Godfrey, and Howdy Doody all together, and connect their freckles with a pencil.
22. Figure out ways to kick an octopus in the tentacles.
23. Write a 10,000 word essay on why Vincent Van Gogh would not have enjoyed stereo.
24. Develop an automatic warning device for your car that buzzes one day before the payment is due.
25. Tattoo a picture of Dom DeLuise on your sternum.
26. See if your English teacher will correct your love letters and give them a grade.
27. Mix LSD with IBM and take a business trip.
28. Knit a parka out of interwoven frankfurter skins.

*　　*　　*

What it means to have a lot of sailors in town—Although it ranks only 18th in population, San Diego leads the nation as the city that gets the most wrong numbers each year.

DOT PUZZLE

This puzzle has been on my desk since I was twelve years old, and I still haven't solved it. My analyst says it is due to a chronic inability to discriminate dots in my imagination from dots in the real world. But then again, my analyst, he's crazy. The answers are on page 117.

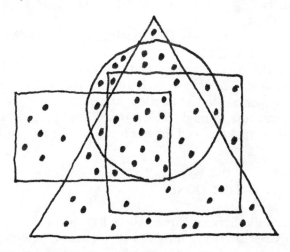

In the diagram above, how many dots are:

1. In the square, but not the triangle, circle or rectangle?
2. In the rectangle, but not the triangle, circle or square?
3. Common to the triangle and circle, but not in the rectangle or square?
4. Common to the square and circle, but not in the triangle or rectangle?
5. Common to the square and rectangle, but not in the circle or triangle?
6. Common to the triangle and rectangle, but not in the circle or square?
7. Common to the triangle, circle and square, but not in the rectangle?
8. Common to the rectangle, square and circle, but not in the triangle?
9. Common to the square, rectangle and triangle, but not in the circle?
10. Common to the circle, square, triangle and rectangle?

Talk is still cheap down on the Bayou

The history of the phone booth began with Thomas B. Doolittle, a Connecticut telegraph man, who opened "pay stations" in Bridgeport and Black Rock in 1878. These were attended telephones, however, not coin boxes. Coin boxes were not introduced until the spring of 1888, after they had been patented by William Gray. Gray's associate, George A. Long, was subsequently responsible for the many improvements that led to the modern pay phone, including the principle of letting coins fall against signal bells to indicate the amount deposited.

The nickel-a-call rate was first established in New York in 1906 and remained until 1951, when it went up to a dime. As AT&T is claiming that the cost of repairs and maintenance, and the demands made on operators necessitate such an increase, there is now talk of another 100% increase in Connecticut and some other states.

All is not yet lost, though. There is still one place in the country where you can make a call in a phone booth for only a nickel: Louisiana.

Cranking up the past

Nevada's Public Service Commission has decided to preserve the Bell System's last surviving magneto (hand-crank) telephone system. The Commission ruled recently that Bell Telephone of Nevada could modernize service in Virginia City, provided that it keeps the magneto crank phones in service as well.

Magneto Wall Telephone c. 1907.

Staying power

New York City's first telephone directory was issued in 1878. It was a small card with a printed list of 271 names. Almost a century later, 44 of the businesses listed in that first directory were still in operation, four of them at the very same address.

They are curious (yellow pages)

AT&T's invitation to "let your fingers do the walking" through the Yellow Pages gets responses from 83.5 million adults in the United States each year. The average user consults the book 43.9 times in a year, usually for information on medical, floral, travel, TV and radio, and home-repair services. According to AT&T, about 93% of Yellow Pages users follow up their consultation with a visit, a letter, or a phone call.

With malice toward none, and accuracy for all except .09%

Yellow Pages for classified directories were first used in 1906 by the Michigan State Telephone Company in Detroit. Today telephone executives claim their listings are 99.91% correct. They *have* to be: businessmen have been known to sue when incorrect listings have caused them to lose business. To win such suits, however, the plaintiff must prove "malicious intent" on the part of the phone company, which is easy to assume but difficult to prove.

* * *

And that's just in paperback—The national bill for printing the country's telephone books comes to about $40 million annually.

© "Ring-a-Ling" Toy Phone & Rubber Duck Co., Inc.

PESTS
PROMPT FREE DELIVERY

SILVERFISH

MOTHS

RATS

FLEAS

CALL

58-211

4 PECK RD., EL MONTE

Living Brain Donors
Discount prices on case lots

Ace Ungrateful Biped Corporation
0 W Las Tunas Dr SGab........289-44

Plastic Surgery
Hare Transplants

Phone & ask for "Bunny" UPdoc23232
King Of Prussia Store   265-510

Propaganda 24 Hrs a Day
Dial 10210608 and Ask for Axis Sally

Rent-A-Pharmacist
To Read Your Favorite Prescription
at Your Next Party — Simply Call
Dr. Jekyl at Hyde Park..........W10

Gorilla Hair Seat Covers
Aabol Cato, 2 Wongneichong Gap Rd H-755361
Aalberts E F, 96 Repulse Bay Rd H-92418
Aamund Asger, 43 Stubbs Rd H-753395

SEALED IN POLY BAGS

DENTAL PLATES
NEW & USED FOR ALL

ETHICAL
RELIABLE

WEDDINGS - DANCES - PARTIES
ALL SPECIAL EVENTS AND EMERGENCIES

24-HR. SERVICE
881-191

Food Things
KENTUCKY FRIED SQUID
Regional Sales Office 72-224

UnMarked Sirloin Steaks
6 NHerkl M00-0000

HERKS RENT-A-PRUNE
For Those
WILD WEEKENDS
in SUN CITY
Add A
DIFFERENT WRINKLE
To Those
OTHERWISE DULL PARTIES

420089Bgldlg Mwd   .OLd 9-534

Saturated Fats
See
Pool Players

State Homes For the Chronically Weird

Home for the Foppish
69 Kreeb St.............M-331017
Home for the Poltroonish
68 Kreeb St.............M-331017
Home for the Giggly
67 Kreeb St.............M-331017
Home for the Oafish
66 Kreeb St.............M-331017
Home for the Greedy
64 Kreeb St.............M-331017
Home for the Incurably Callous
63 Kreeb St.............M-331017
Home for the Loutish
62 Kreeb St.............M-331017
Home for the Ofay
61 Kreeb St.............M-331017
Home for the Shifty
60 Kreeb St.............M-331017
Home for the Nastyminded
59 Kreeb St.............M-331016

Dear John Letters
DRAFT DODGERS INC.
Send Your
TEN YEAR OLD
to
CANADA
Keep Him Out of
THE BOY SCOUTS
From Orange County   889-800

Jewelry-Whsle
Jewelry Buyers
Jewelry Thieves
Squeeking Pips for Your Favorite
Pipsqueek   333PpskwkR

Elephant Decoys
Dandruff-Whsle & Mfrs
Gabor Sisters
Filthy Movies
24 HRS. A DAY

Corner of
Santa Monica Blvd.
& Everywhere
Phone Number for
Current Listing
(Use Assumed Voice)

99

Shills
To Play Parking Meters
on Slow Streets

HOUSE OF NOISE

TELEFUNKEN
OTHERFUNKEN

SONNY
CHER

HIS MASTER'S VICE

For Information—Call Me
irresponsible

SHYSTER SOUND
Plotz & Keck St Mtchll SD. 88-888

SINCE 1944
CESSPOOL
& SEPTIC TANK
PATROL

ETHICAL   RELIABLE
& ASSOCIATES
2925 Riverside Dr ShOks. 872-210

Yalo
Pages

UNINFORMED
ARMED GUARDS

"SINCE 1956"

Protecting Your

House
Factory
Business Place
Watchdog
Trees

FOONMAN'S GUARD SERVICE

Call
10-4

BREET'S
RENTALS

FLOORS • RUGS • WALLS • METAL

LEASE PURCHASE
PLAN

For Every Occasion

Camping   Guest Needs
Andy Warhol   Beds
Tiffany Lamps   Oxygen
Snooky Lanson   Tools

33 Vally ElM. 444-231

DISHWASHERS

Our Dishwashers Include—
Mr. Earl C. Festoon
Ms. Selma Preltz
Mr. Jim Miller

GREBTZ APPLIANCES

Another myth shattered

Contrary to popular belief, it was a Canadian who invented the telephone. Alexander Graham Bell did not become a citizen of the United States until November 10, 1882. When he had applied for citizenship eight years earlier, he was denied it.

Old Father Hubbard

When Bell fell in love with Mabel Hubbard, the 15-year-old daughter of a Boston lawyer, he asked her father for permission to marry her. "If you wish to marry my daughter," Hubbard told Bell, "you must abandon your foolish telephone." Fortunately, however, Hubbard abandoned his foolish notion and subsequently became one of Bell's financial backers.

They're still gross

By August of 1877, when Bell's patent was only 16 months old, 778 telephones were already in use. The company was owned entirely by the inventor and his two backers, each with 30% of the stock, and Bell's assistant, Watson, who had 10%. By this time, Bell was selling magneto sets at the rate of a thousand a month, and by 1881 there were 1,200 towns on the Bell Telephone map. A year later, the phone company achieved gross earnings in six figures.

... and a few other things we could mention

Author Gay Talese once suggested that "the telephone was invented several years after the bathtub, giving considerable support to the belief that the telephone is an instrument of the devil put on earth to interrupt long, warm baths."

MATCHLESS MIND READING

Ask your telephone friend to pull any number of matches from a full book and, after a little hanky panky, you can tell him how many he has in his hand.

Have him remove from a full book of 20 matches any number less than 10 and place them in his pocket. Now tell him to count the matches remaining in the folder, add the two digits, and tear out enough matches to equal the total of the two digits. These matches he should also place in his pocket.

For example, if he originally tore out 9 matches, 11 would remain. The total of the two digits (1+1=2) is two; therefore two more matches would be removed from the folder and placed in his pocket. If 12 matches remain (1+2=3), three are placed in the pocket. If 13 remain, four are placed in the pocket.

Finally, tell him to tear out any number or all the remaining matches, hold them in his fist, and tell you how many matches are still in the folder. Subtract that number from nine and you will know the number of matches he has in his closed hand. Of course, if no matches remain in the book, your friend must have nine matches in his hand.

Dial O for !!!

Operators get about 30,000 calls a year from people who need help and are too confused or imperilled to call the police, fire department, rescue squad, or other agency. Even if you have time only to shout "Help!" to an operator, she is plugged into your line and can have a switchman trace the call back to its origin. Following the trunk line from her board, she locates the closed contacts with a code number that can be looked up to find your address.

Buttoning up the human factors

Bell Laboratories in Murray Hill, New Jersey, has a Human Factors Engineering group headed by research psychologists who spend all of their time figuring out things like what sort of buttons the push-button phone should have. John E. Karlin, Ph. D., was responsible for that particular project. Dr. Karlin was the man who, earlier, had come up with the idea of putting the numbers *outside* the dial wheel. Also, as experiments had proved that people tended to dial more efficiently when they had some target for their fingers, Karlin had introduced the dial with white dots inside each hole.

When the push-button phone was in its developmental stages, Karlin was consulted again. Push-button phones, he says, "look simple enough, but the truth is, they bristle with scores of fascinating technological and psychological problems." Karlin and his crew studied 38 "human factor variables in three categories" before settling on the design for the phone.

In the first category were the possible patterns in which the buttons were to be arranged. Polling people at random, they received all sorts of suggestions: triangles, half-moons, and crosses were among them, but tested out poorly for speed, accuracy, and even the way users felt about them. In the end, they chose the familiar three-rows-of-three-buttons with one at the bottom for "O" because it "seemed best from an engineering point of view."

Second, they asked questions about "force displacements." How far should the buttons project from the surface? How far should they move? How much force should one have to exert to get them into motion?

The third category included the shape of the buttons and other miscellaneous factors. How big should the buttons be? Should they be concave or convex, flat or round, matte-finished or glossy, rectangular or square?

"Our job was to state the human-factor requirements for the best possible push button," says Karlin, "and we're pretty sure that nobody on earth knows more about them than we do."

Paging Gertrude

A record number of telephone directories disappeared into the ticker-tape parade for swimmer Gertrude Ederle in New York in 1926, after she swam the English Channel. The pages of 5,000 phone books were showered on her. It cost $2,000 to replace all the directories.

Banking with Bell

Some of the phone companies that collect used directories from their subscribers have inspectors go through the old books and remove the things people have left inside them. Many subscribers, it seems, use the directory as a combination safe deposit box and bureau drawer. They press neckties in directories and stash everything from love letters to savings bonds. The inspectors find deeds, wedding certificates, stamp collections, lottery tickets, insurance policies, trading stamps and, sometimes, money. In 1954, for instance, a New York directory inspector turned a page and found a $100 bill.

Once a New England storekeeper tucked away his Saturday receipts of $1,500 in his office phone book, only to return on Monday to find that it had been carted away earlier that morning. The phone company told him that he was welcome to come down and search through the collected directories—all 100,000 of them. Enlisting the aid of his wife, sister, brother-in-law, and two nephews, he did just that. Three days and 75,000 phone books later, he found the cash.

Ilka Chase once said, "America's best buy for a nickel is a telephone call to the right man."

How's the weather up there?

Leo Rosten, author of *The Education of Hyman Kaplan,* tells the joke about a man who was astonished to read his own obituary in the morning paper. He called his lawyer and asked, "Hello, Irwin? Have you seen this morning's paper?"

"Sure. Who is this?"

"What do you mean 'Who is this'? It's *me*—Jack. I want you to sue . . ."

"*Jack?*" cried the lawyer.

"Of course! I want you to . . ."

"Jack, where are you calling from?"

PHONEY OVER-THE-PHONE PHONEBOOK READING

Here are a couple of number tricks (or tricky numbers) by which you can predict the word "chosen" by a friend from his phonebook. It always works as long as your friend knows how to add and subtract.

Tell a phone friend to write down any number—say 137. Add a zero to that number to make it 1370. Subtract original number (1370 - 137) and get 1233. Add the digits of this answer (1+2+3+3), and your friend will always arrive at nine.

Since this number seems to have been freely arrived at by your friend, and he doesn't know that you know it, you are ready to perform an apparent miracle.

Tell your friend to open the phonebook to the page of the number he has "freely chosen." It will, of course, always be page nine. Open your phonebook to the same page.

Now tell your friend that if he will concentrate on the first name in the left-hand column, you will read his mind and tell him what it is.

When you have performed this trick successfully, and he asks you to "do it again"—and he will—don't use the same number pattern or he might catch on. Instead, do the following "number force," which always results in an 18.

Tell your friend on the other end of the line to write down any three digits. If the second is bigger than the first, the third must be bigger than the second. If the second is smaller than the first, the third must be smaller than the second.

Example: 179 or 971.

Reverse the numbers and subtract smaller from larger (971 - 179 = 792). Add the digits of the result of the subtraction (7+9+2), and the final number will always equal 18.

The following numbers (198, 297, 396, 495, 594, 693, 792, 891) are the only answers a person can get before he adds the digits at the end of the subtraction. The middle number is always nine. You can use that fact to make your prediction more mysterious and not only predict the first name on page eighteen, but you can have your friend (or ex-friend) look at the page and count down to another name. Example: if his answer is 198, have him look at page 19 and then count down to the eighth name. All you need do is ask the person to tell you the first number. By subtracting the first number (one) from the middle number (always nine), you can figure out the last number (eight). Another example; if the first digit is six, you know nine is the middle digit, the last digit must be three. If the first digit is five, then the last digit is four, and the number is 594.

Now you can not only tell him the name at the top, but also any name that can be derived from the numbers on the above list.

The patter of little voices

Remember rainy days when your mother wasn't home, before TV and message unit calls, how you and your friends would get together and make life miserable for a few randomly chosen fellow telephone subscribers? Or a few unfortunate people from the phone book who happened to have names like Fox? (Hello, are you Mr. Fox? ... Yes ... Well, I've got three chickens in my yard—would you come over and eat them?)

1. Is your refrigerator running?
   Better go catch it.
2. Is your house on the bus line?
   Get it off because there's a bus coming!
3. Do you have Prince Albert in the can?
   Tell him to get out because we have to use the bathroom.
4. Hello. Is this the Game Warden?
   Yes, it is.
   Oh good! What would you suggest for my kid's birthday party?
5. Hello. We're taking a survey. Did you ever see a catfish?
   Yes.
   How does it hold the pole?
6. Hello. We're taking a survey. Did you ever see a horsefly?
   Yes.
   He must have had a big pair of pants!

7. Hello. Do you have dry onions?
   Yes.
   Well, give them a drink!
8. Hello and happy birthday. I want to buy you a new handkerchief. What's the size of your nose?
9. Leave a call for a friend, saying a Mr. Wolfe called, then leave the number of the zoo.

AT&T reports that there are no significant regional variations in number of complaints about nuisance calls. Investigations in New York have also revealed that 65% of all nuisance calls are made by children who are "just having fun."

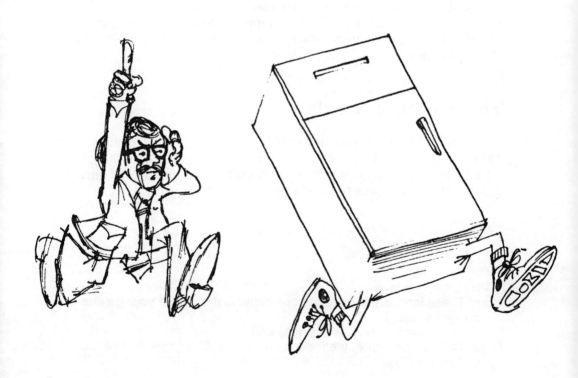

The Smith System

In Falls Church, Virginia, people like to point out a riverside residence, which they refer to as "The House Ma Bell Built." No, it's not the home of an AT&T executive, although the owners did once run a company by the name of The Bell System.

Mr. and Mrs. Raymond L. Smith of Washington, D.C. had an answering service by that name, and their logo was the familiar blue-and-white handset on phone booths all over America. The Smiths registered the symbol and company name in 1953. That was more than the phone company had done, for Bell's attorneys discovered to their horror that year that the Bell System logo and trade name had never been registered!

The dispute could have gone to court and lasted for years, but both sides were reasonable. The Smiths traded their logo for an $18,000 home, whereupon Bell applied for, and received rights to, the words "Bell System" and the logo.

That's a lot of people

In 1972, AT&T employed 1,000,772 people (199 more than in 1971). This means that, even if 95% of its employees are on the job on a given day, there are still over 50,000 people absent—a figure equal to the entire work force of a medium-sized city.

* * *

Boss: These long-distance telephone conversations with your friends have got to stop!
Secretary: It was ... er ... a business call.
Boss: Well, in the future, please remember this firm never addresses its clients as "Hi, stud!"

But aren't you glad you can use the dial?
Don't you wish everybody did?

When the dial system was introduced in Washington, D.C., in 1930, Senator Carter Glass attempted to push a resolution through Congress to ban the dial. "I object to being transformed into an employee of the phone company without compensation," he said.

Doesn't it make you nervous when you call Dial-A-Prayer and the number has been disconnected?

The informants

The life of an information operator is not an easy one. Operators have to keep track of thousands of numbers, those in the bulky white directories, plus a daily addendum containing up to 500 new names and numbers. (Information receives word of new subscribers within 24 hours of connection.) In addition, operators have to memorize at least 25 frequently called numbers, including those of airlines, bus and train terminals, clinics and hospitals, and department stores. They take calls in automatic rotation, while supervisors roam the corridors behind their glass-partitioned booths, occasionally checking up on them by plugging their headsets into the switchboards.

At the tone . . .

Jane Barbe will tell you the time in 250 American cities. She has been called "the greatest recording star in the history of the planet," because she is the one who records the time of the day for Audichron, the company whose "time machines" are used by the Bell System. AT&T estimates that Jane Barbe has given out the time over 100 million times.

Going Nutts

Two former telegraph operators, Emma M. Nutt and her sister Stella, became the first women telephone operators on September 1, 1878, in Boston. Gradually thereafter women were brought in to replace the teen-age boys who had manned the switchboards up until then. The women were considered easier to train, more conscientious, and much more likely to give the "soft answer that turneth away wrath." By 1890 women operated nearly all of Bell's daytime switchboards, and by the turn of the century they had taken over the night shifts as well.

*   *   *

Some enterprising (but sexist) statistician in the phone company once produced the calculation that, had the company not converted to automatic switching equipment, by now every woman in the United States would be needed to man, or rather, work at the switchboards as operators.

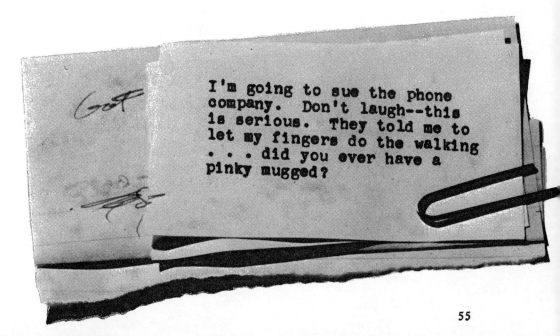

I'm going to sue the phone company. Don't laugh--this is serious. They told me to let my fingers do the walking . . . did you ever have a pinky mugged?

Cowed into silence

Early rural telephone wires were strung across just about anything that was standing—not only telephone poles, but windmills, silos, and even fence posts. In fact, it was fairly common for phone conversations to sputter and die out as a result of cattle rubbing against the fence lines.

Wanted urgently: 34,000 very tall men

In December, 1924, a sleet storm knocked down 34,000 telephone poles in Missouri, Kansas, Oklahoma, and Texas. Emergency restoration took only ten days, but complete restoration took several months.

Your 12 years are up

The average life expectancy of a telephone pole is 12 years. Most telephone poles are made from cedars, chestnuts, or junipers—and the trees aren't usually considered poleworthy until they reach the age of 60. In 1910, there were enough poles in the Bell System to cover an area the size of Rhode Island, but nowadays the phone company considers them obsolete and they're being replaced by underground cables wherever possible. A few of the obsolete poles, however, were left standing in Arizona—birds were nesting in the crossbeams.

No pole-ish jokes please!

Obscene calls

Only about 20% of all nuisance calls are actually obscene, and studies have shown that most of these are made by men under 30 who either hate or fear women.

Dozens of stratagems have been devised to thwart obscene phone callers. Two of the most popular:

Blow a shrill whistle into the mouthpiece, which will at least give the caller an earache.

Place a tape recorder next to the phone with a pre-recorded "beep" like those used on radio and TV shows to indicate that calls are being recorded.

Or you could try
a little heavy breathing of your own

1. Always answer the phone by saying, "Hello . . . who the hell is this?" (That will catch him off guard and, in the spirit of one-up-manship, you will have won! Plus, if this is the phrase that the radio station running a contest wants to hear, you may win something.)
2. Pick up your phone slowly and give a loud raspberry into the mouthpiece.
3. Answer your phone using the Lithuanian language. This will confuse the obscene caller unless, of course, he is also Lithuanian.
4. You could say, "Police Headquarters. Surly and mean Captain Zernman talking."
5. If you believe the obscene caller to be elderly, talk about things that will interest him, like Deanna Durbin movies and the Chrysler Airflow, and maybe his Russ Columbo records.

Some non-obscene things
you can say to an obscene caller

No thanks, we already subscribe to the *Times*.

Just a second while I get a smoke.

Let me get my sister on the other phone. She's a voyeuse.

I hope you don't get in any trouble for this. You know the Vice Squad's tapping my line.

Have you ever considered writing dirty books? You could make a fortune in porno.

We've got a bad connection. Hang up and I'll call you right back.

Lt. Sloan, I think it's *him* again.

You've got the wrong number. We get calls for the Sanitation Department all the time.

Say, glad to meet you. I'm an old obscene phone caller myself.

Say two *Our Fathers*
and I'll call you in the morning

As in burlesque, in obscene phone calling "you gotta have a gimmick." One of the most imaginative gimmicks ever devised was that of the infamous "Father Steiner," who phoned women in New Jersey in 1964. He would call up and ask if the victim happened to be Catholic and, if the answer was yes, he would launch his "confession" spiel, saying the woman's phone number had been left at the switchboard of a local Catholic university. "The message says you've asked for a confession. This is Father Steiner and I'm ready to hear it."

Now the sacrament of penance is never administered by telephone, but many women went along with the ruse. "Father Steiner's" questions grew increasingly personal and increasingly more related to sexual habits: "How many times have you had relations with your husband this past week?" "Have you had relations with anyone else in this period?" And so on. The questions gradually became more intimate and more embarrassing.

Before the police could track him down, he had made thousands of calls, as many as 135 in one 24-hour period. "Father Steiner" turned out to be a 25-year-old businessman, married, and the father of two.

"I don't know why I did it," he said. "I guess I need help."

The calls of St. Paul

St. Paul, Minnesota, has had more than its share of telephone terrorists. One of the most notorious used the "survey" gimmick to get information out of his victims—information they wouldn't normally give to a stranger. He identified himself as a newspaper reporter, which always seemed to flatter his female victims. Then from each he would learn whether her husband worked nights and, if so, *which* nights. Such information, of course, is invaluable to burglars, muggers, peeping Toms, and others, but a police spokesman said "You'd be surprised how many ladies volunteered these facts."

Also in St. Paul, there was an infamous "undergarment salesman" who would call and ask for the ladies' measurements. "You wouldn't believe it," said the city's Vice Squad chief, "but most of the women who've complained to us have actually given their measurements." As an inducement, he pointed out, the "salesman" promised a free gift—a set of expensive underwear.

WORD CHESS

This is a game like "WORD SQUARES" (page 89), but somewhat more complicated.

First you and your phone friend must draw up a box with 25 squares and then, calling out letters alternately going from the top row, the second row, the third row, the fourth row, the fifth row all left to right, fill in the boxes so that you both have cards exactly alike.

The game is to see which of you can make more four-letter words out of the letters in front of you, moving from one box to another in any direction you wish.

After you have the cards made out, agree on the time limit for the game, and hang up. Then call back. At this point, each player should announce how many words he has found. The one who has found the most is the winner. Each player can verify the accuracy of the other's words by looking at his own card.

It's important that at least 30% of the letters on the board be vowels; try to include all the vowels and Y. A great many variations are possible in setting up the rules, such as whether a person can use the same letter twice in the same word. Another way to vary the rules is to limit the moves that can be made in order to get to the next letter. For instance, one could be allowed two vertical moves, three diagonal moves, one move like a chess knight, etc.

The pause that's recycled

TASI, or Time Assignment Speech Interpolation, is a means of sandwiching several conversations together on one channel or line. It was created for use on the transatlantic cable, whose 36 channels (each way) can be doubled with the equipment.

Bell engineers call the "active" or "speaking" moments in a phone conversation "talkspurts." In between talkspurts are pauses and silences when nothing is said—for instance, between the time some-one asks a question and the moment it's answered at the other end. TASI robs these silences, snipping them out for use by other transatlantic callers.

Here's how it works. Until the thirty-seventh conversation comes in, TASI sits by patiently, its transistors, diodes, and circuitry awaiting their cue. When call 37 hits the line, TASI springs into action, shifting talkspurts from channel to channel and borrowing the silences for use by the thirty-seventh caller. During busy hours, talks get shifted from channel to channel, tucked into the "spaces" between talkspurts.

There are occasional "freeze-outs," when a talkspurt has nowhere to go and must be held to await available channel space. But the law of averages is such that only one talkspurt in about 10,000 will be frozen out for as long as a quarter of a second. When this happens, about two syllables of speech are clipped out and lost forever. Supposedly, this happens about once in every 30 calls during the peak traffic hours.

Something similar occurs on some long-distance calls between points *within* the continental United States. Pulse-code modulation and signal-splitting equipment help increase the number of calls that can be made on a single long-distance line. Special carrier systems divide the frequency bandwidth to accommodate several calls at once.

Top ten talkers

Listed below are the ten talkingest nations on earth. The figures refer to the average number of conversations per person each year.

United States	830
Canada	781
Sweden	687
Iceland	639
Barbados	535
Bahamas	483
Bermuda	449
Japan	400
Denmark	398
Singapore	366

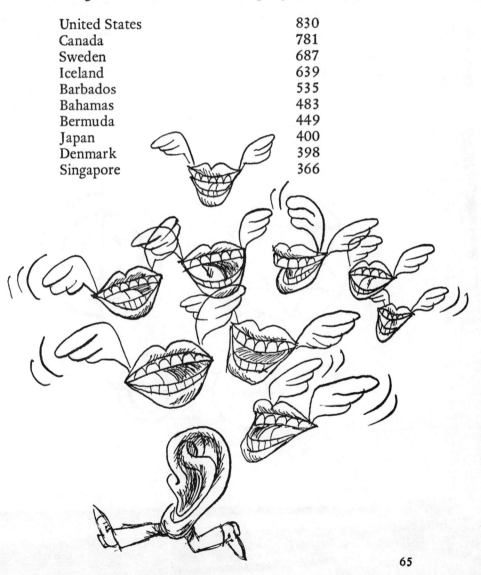

STUNTS WITH A PENCIL

There are times when you simply have to be a good listener—but listening need involve only your telephone ear. Here's how the rest of you can have a good time while you're sharing someone's troubles. Just see if you can trace these figures in one continuous line without crossing any lines or lifting your pencil from the paper. It may be fun, but it's not easy! You'll find the solutions to these brain-ticklers on page 117.

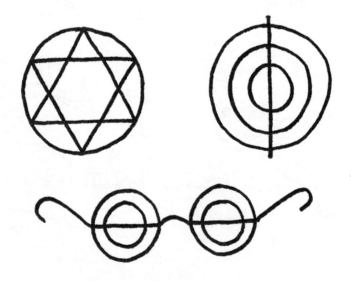

The babble belt

In 1892, the first long-distance service was inaugurated between New York and Chicago. In 1912, it was extended to Denver and, in 1915, to California. The link-up from coast to coast went across 13 states and 130,000 telephone poles.

At one time it was BETTER than being there

Long distance, we are told, is "the next best thing to being there." Back in 1909, when 18,000 calls were placed daily between New York and Chicago (earning Bell $22,000 seven times a week), a special Long Distance Salon was opened in Manhattan. To entice paying customers and get them into the "long-distance habit," the New York Telephone Company sent taxis to pick them up and bring them to the salon, whereupon they were escorted over Oriental carpets to a gilded booth draped with silk curtains.

Doing it the hard way

On April 25, 1935, the first round-the-world phone call was made over a 23,000-mile circuit of wire and radio channels. The call was made by Walter S. Gifford, president of AT&T, to one of his vice-presidents, T. G. Miller. The two men were in separate offices only a few feet away from each other.

Tired of talking to the same old people?

A three-minute person-to-person call to Peking costs $12 ($9 for station-to-station.) For $12 you can also call Tierra del Fuego, Saigon, Bombay, Calcutta, or Petropavlovsk, Siberia. A call to Timbuktu will set you back $15.

How to get off the phone

All of us have had to endure the difficult experience of the telephone sales pitch, delivered by a salesperson who has been carefully trained in how not to take "no" for an answer. The more undesirable the merchandise, the more skillful the pitch. Here, at last, are some carefully researched and proven methods for getting free of such calls.

1. Excuse me, but I've got to get off the phone. A group of enraged pygmies is climbing over me.
2. I have to finish knitting a slipcover for my diving board.
3. I have to eviscerate my avocado with a dull shoehorn before four o'clock.
4. I have to finish stomping on the tarantulas before Queen Elizabeth arrives.
5. I have to go out and get my baby pictures retouched.
6. Mr. Peanut has stolen my Shell credit card and I have to phone the police.
7. I have to go over to the real estate office and take my wife out of escrow!

W.p.m.—New York Telephone has come up with the fascinating information that, if you are a slow speaker, you will average 450 words in a three-minute call and, if you talk quickly, you can get in about 750 words. This means that in one three-mintue call you could recite both Lincoln's Gettysburg Address and the "To Be or Not To Be" soliloquy from *Hamlet* (a total of 530 words) without even hurrying.

Going for a song

In 1912, when the phrase "The Voice with a Smile" came into the Bell System's PR phraseology, operators were required to be "in good health, quick-handed, clear-voiced, poised, and alert." Really good operators often found themselves called upon to play numerous roles: detectives, confessors, mind-readers, psychologists, and hand-holders. Popular songs from those early days bore witness to the high expectations generated by the operators.

At the turn of the century, it was "My Love Is a Telephone Girl"; in 1901, "Hello Central, Give Me Heaven"; later, "Ring Me Up Heaven, Central"; in 1913, "Please Central, Find Me My Mama;" and during World War One, "Hello Central, Get Me No-Man's-Land."

PHONEY MAGIC

Here is a trick by which your telephone friend can pick any card from a full deck, and you can tell him which card he has chosen.

Tell him to shuffle a deck of cards and to stop any time he wishes. Then ask him to look at the bottom card of the pack and remember it. Figuring that the Jack equals 11, the Queen 12, and the King 13, he should take the number value of the card he has chosen and move that many cards from the top of the deck to the bottom of the deck.

Now, tell him to hold the cards facing himself and read off one card at a time slowly. As he reads off the first card, stop him and ask, "Did you cut the deck?" When he says "no," ask him to put the card back and then cut the deck.

You must remember the card he called out (the first one facing him) before you ask him to make the cut.

Now tell him to hold the pack so that he can read off the cards from the bottom, one at a time *slowly,* and warn him not to stop or indicate by his voice which card he originally chose.

As soon as you hear him call out the card he called out before making the cut, start counting to yourself from one to 13 as he reads through the next 13 cards. As soon as the number on the card he reads coincides with the number you are counting, you will know the card he has chosen, i.e., when he comes to the fifth card and its number is also five, that will be the card he originally chose. For added effectiveness, it's wise to let fully 13 cards pass.

Sometimes by chance not just one but two cards in the run of 13 will coincide. In that case, you can eliminate one by asking if the card was red or black, high or low, odd or even.

"Take a Ride on the Penn Central"

The Lake Erie Telephone & Telegraph Co.

Gymnasium Equipment

Cranes

Storks

Kiwis

Orthopedic Supplies

Eyebrows That Can Be Used
as Bent Fenders

GAMEKEEPERS FOR RENT
  Mr. Mellors Chatterly Estate
  London 28, Eng. OI-443 262

Unusual Products

  Fill Your Freezer with Wet
  Advertising Throwaways from
  Sandra Dee's Lawn.
    24-Hour-A-Day Number..........1959
      Ask for "Creepo"

"Help!—I'm Trapped inside This Linotype

Would You Like to See Marlin Perkins
Attempt to catch a Moth with Only
Some Dentures in His Hand??
      Dial ZOO—Ask for Mr. Byrd

Aquariums

DINERS GLUB

HOUSE OF GLUB, INC.

HADDOCKS (Take Two Aspirin & Call Me
      in the Morning)

ROBERT TROUT
  Want Fish Who Will Work for Scale?

Play Bridge with a Porpoise Or Under
One with Your Favorite Snorkler!

Women Eating Sharks

Mortuaries

ZERNMAN'S DEATH CITY
  2 EForestLwn Rsmd....RIp7-77899
  (Please See Advertisement This Page)

STIFFO'S
  2 WFoerstLwn Lwndle.RIp77-7899

Great Beyond Inc.
  6ApianWy RO1-1OVER
  2 NFoorstLn SGab..........RIp-9987

Call For Rigor Mortis
  2SFrstLw RIp6-7798

  OVER 40 YEARS EXPERIENCE IN THE
  EVALUATING AND PURCHASING OF
  JEWELRY - DIAMONDS AND ART OBJECTS

▶ **Diaper Service**

SNARFMYER'S DIAPER SERVICE
For the Wetter Forecast
  .... Dial FI2-333333

CA-CA INC.
Satisfaction since 1483
Personalized Diapers Back In Hours
  No.1PotteeLn PP6-0099

Old Newscasters

Freezers—Cryogenics

  Song Titles For Silly People

"Freezer Jolly Good Fellow"

CHECKS & CREDIT ACCEPTED

443-869

24 HOURS

SERVING

ALL JAILS

"BORIS"

ABC TV Network
  Cor MontyHall&DellaSt
ABC Alphabet Co.
  Dial 123 and say "Hewwo?"
A-Loverly Bunch of Coconuts
  Merv Griffen
A-TRAIN Duke Ellington
APEX Apex Bad Boy is not difficult to
  find throughout literature
ACE HOLE CO. Augering in a new year
          of Rooting for our team
AMF Pinafore
Sour Washcloths for rent or for
  Destroying 55NHdsn........TU6-669

FLYING SAUCER

飛碟牌

內襯 衣筋 領內操衣筋 玩具 國際阿襯
海游 頭水襟 膠力 具筋筋
等塑彈 麻襟筋 麻

PRODUCTS:
RUBBER BANDS FOR GARMENT, PLASTIC,
WIGS-MAKER FACTORY USES, ETC.

HOP CHUNG RUBBER BAND MFY.

FOK SING FTY. BLDG., BLOCK 12, 2, WALNUT ST., G/F.,
TAI KOK TSUI, KOWLOON

TELS: K-920411, K-942397

G

SERVICE ON DIVORCE EVIDENCE

FREE 2-HR VISIT

Synthetic Humility
1MoleCt. TY2-888888

Delicacies
Baked Storm Door—Imported
    From Lawrence Kansas
Baked Accordion—Imported
    From Lawrence Welk

KRELMANS
EVERYTHING FOR EVERYBODY

SALES - SERVICE - ACCESSORIES

Easy Terms •

• FACTORY PARTS
• TRAINED MECHANICS

WE ALSO REPAIR & REPLACE

Electric Foons
Spray Gredneys

Deebs
Pelfings   **74-1525**

FAST KREEBLEMYER PARK CROLMOBILE

AUTHORIZED LEASING
SALES • SERVICE

243-456

SEE THE 1974
CROLMOBILE
It Has A Sunfloor

FOONMAN MORTUARY
& MASSAGE PARLOR

24 HOUR SERVICE

GASKETS - HANDLES - LOCKS
CALL ANYTIME
INCLUDING SUNDAYS & HOLIDAYS

Embossing
Embalming
Embalming-Embossers
Used Soup
DR. BOB KNOZ

For A
NOSE 'BOB'

AVOID EMBARRASEMENT
DISCOUNT PRICES on CASE LOTS

Embossing Embalmers
Rhinocerous Hide Whips
Licorice Whips
Senate Majority Whips
Lash Larue

LETTER DOODLES

Let's face it—Salvador Dali you're not. Without saying so, people probably look down on you for those arrows, boxes, and lopsided circles that fill your scratch pad. Here are some instructions from Gary Owens' Infamous Doodlers School that will make you seem more creative than you really are.

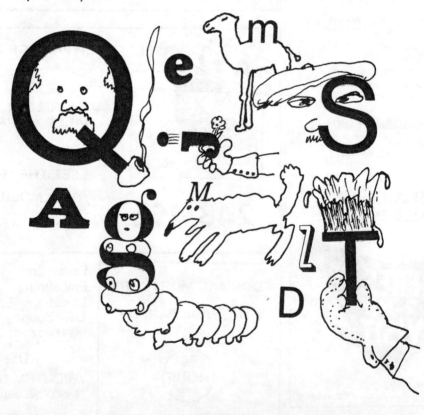

Your number's up

Harold S. Osborne, a former Bell chief engineer, has described what AT&T probably sees as the final stage in the telephonizing of America: "At birth, a baby is given a telephone number for life. Later, when he wishes to talk to anyone in the world, he will pull out a watch-like device with ten little buttons on one side and a screen on the other. He will punch the number on the keys; then, turning the device over, he will hear the voice of his friend and see his face on the screen, in color, and in three dimensions."

Osborne adds, "If he does not see him and hear him, he will know that his friend is dead."

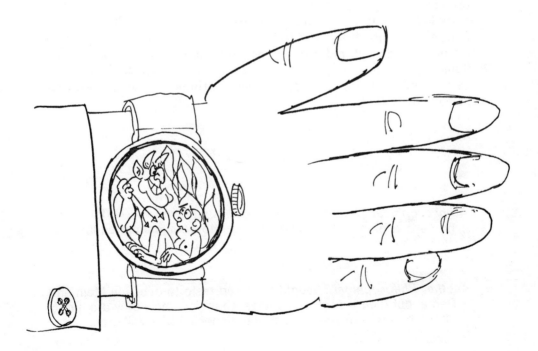

Non-answering service

In New York City, there's never an answer at 687-9970. It rings and rings but it's never answered. The same is true of 755-5099. This is because they're both dummy numbers—numbers that Broadway, Hollywood, TV, and writers use when they need a phone number for the purposes of fiction. Judy Holliday used one of these in *Bells Are Ringing*—remember "Plaza O double O double 3"?

Woe to the person who uses his own number in a movie, play, or story. Consider the sad case of the Manhattan cartoonist who used his own phone number in a drawing published in a national magazine. Within two hours after the issue hit the newsstands, his wife was obliged to answer more than 100 calls from the magazine's readers.

In 1952, 82 dummy phone numbers were issued for dramatic and fictional purposes: 48 went to TV shows, 15 to the movies, nine to cartoonists, nine to radio programs, and one to a short story writer. Some movie companies have been using one particular dummy for years. Universal, for example, wouldn't think of parting with its beloved 877-5098.

*　*　*

A Philosophical Thought: A true friend is one who will nudge you if he sees a giant killer squid getting into your enema equipment.

*　*　*

Another Philosophical Thought: It is bad taste to question Mom and Dad about their insurance policies when you know they are jumpy about the tire iron you carry to the dinner table. —Voltaire

If a machine answers, don't hang up

Since machines are taking over the world, we must help them cultivate a sense of humor. So, the next time somebody's answering machine says "hello" to you, give it a laugh:

Hi there! This is_____. We want you to call us as soon as possible. Sir Edmund Hillary and I are planning to climb Raquel Welch this afternoon . . . just because she's there. You can reach us at_____.

Hello, this is_____. I'm calling to remind you we'll be at the Jolly Green Giant's house defrosting his niblets!
My number is_____.
My hat size is_____.
My social security number is_____.
Myopia is nearsightedness.

Hello, this is_____. I'm recorded now. If you wish to call me back when you play your recording, I'll be at_____. From 4 o'clock on I will be home and able to talk to you live.
This is a recording. Thank you . . . thank you . . . thank you. . . .

Hi! _____ and I are going to go over and try to get on "Let's Make A Deal." She's dressing as a duck and I'm going as a vegetable. Because of your personality we thought you could be a fruit. Give us a call at_____.

Hello! This is "Lucky Telephone Time!" It's too bad you weren't home just now. But our jackpot, which includes $100,000 a year for life, a Boeing 747 at your disposal twenty-four hours a day for the next ten years, and a free flashlight will go to the next person who answers our call. Tough luck fella! If you want to complain just call_____.

Department of dirty tricks

There are a number of schemes by which subscribers deprive AT&T of millions of dollars each year.

There is, for example, the "No Answer Code." A man calls his wife at a prearranged time, letting her know which commuter train he's going to be on by the number of times he lets the phone ring before hanging up. She's expecting the call, of course, so she doesn't answer, but she gets all the information she needs without paying the toll. Then there is the collect call routine, by which the commuting husband calls person-to-person and leaves word for a fictitious party to call him back at, say, 6:20. The wife knows that her husband is on the 6:20 train home. Another gimmick is the "Safe Arrival Code." When a traveler gets to where he's going, he calls person-to-person and asks to speak to himself. Naturally, his wife says, "He's not here." And now she knows where "he" is and that he's arrived safe and sound.

Even businesses resort to such schemes. For instance, a ball-bearing manufacturer in Pittsburgh may call a distributor in Dallas and ask for "Mr. Hemphill" (code name for a certain size of bearing.) If the distributor says "Hemphill" isn't in but will be back on "the fifteenth," it is notification of an order of 15 cases of "Hemphills."

Illinois Bell Telephone estimated that it loses $400,000 annually on tricks such as these. One of the main reasons the phone company doesn't prosecute such cases—even if it could catch the offenders—is that publicity would give thousands of subscribers ingenious new cheating ideas.

*   *   *

The favorite song of telephone buggers is taps.

Don't bet on it

A large percentage of your income tax is spent by the federal government on the tapping of lines. Federal agencies tapped 500,000 of them in 1971 alone. On the basis of these taps, a grand total of 300 convictions was obtained. In 1970, 380,000 taps resulted in 538 convictions, and in 1969, 170,000 taps yielded 294 guilty verdicts. There were no convictions at all in 1968.

The government estimates that 90% of the wiretapping is to track down gambling offenses.

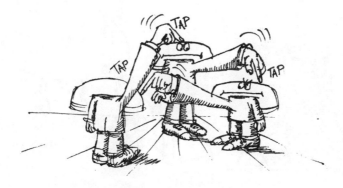

Legs & Lucky & Waxey & Dutch

Professional wire-tapper William J. Mellin's specialty was underworld overlords. He tapped, during his long career, "Lucky" Luciano, "Legs" Diamond, Arnold Rothstein, "Waxey" Wexler, and Joe Adonis, among many others. Mellin's favorite tap victim was "Dutch" Schultz, who suspected his calls were being monitored and ripped his phone off the wall in a fit of temper. When associates informed Schultz that merely disconnecting the phone would not undo the tap, he had the desk set reconnected. From then on he closed his phone conversations with a few words for the tapper: "Mellin, you dumb Dutchman, I know you're listening. I hope your ears fall off."

Why it's unlikely that your phone is bugged—
unless you're really up to something interesting:

If the government wants to listen in on your conversations, the agents involved must present a request to tap your phone to a U.S. attorney. The matter is then passed on directly to the U.S. attorney general, who must personally approve the request. (Once a case was thrown out in Florida when it was pointed out that not John Mitchell but one of his assistants had initialed the request to tap.) The request then is taken before a federal judge for final approval.

But for the tap to provide legally useful evidence, there should be:

1. twenty-four hour monitoring for as long as the tap is in place
2. two people manning at least two recorders at all times
3. two cars, each with two people inside, watching the bugged location from the outside
4. an interpreter, if there is a foreign language being used
5. a transcriber to type out the conversations.

This means at least seven people involved at all times, or twenty-one people per day (three shifts).

All this adds up to a monstrous expense—$100,000 a month or thereabouts—so you have to be worth it.

If someone close to you wants to know what you're saying and to whom, they must be both rich and a little reckless. The penalty for tapping a phone without the attorney general's permission is five years and/or $10,000 (though at last report most first offenders were only spending about six months in jail).

To install any kind of decent tap, an "electronic surveillance expert" must be hired. These people are very hard to find, they are paid in cash, and they make about $100,000 a year working free-lance. Are they overpaid? One expert, whom we can't name, says that each job is a complex engineering problem, since the bug's transmitter must compete with radio stations, police or citizens' band radios, and other radio "pollution" in the neighborhood. Each transmitter must be custom-built by someone who knows what he's doing.

Nor is the equipment cheap. The simplest devices start at $500, and they go up in the thousands depending on performance, quality, features, etc.

What if you think your phone is tapped?

Call the phone company and talk to a service representative. Within a couple of days a technician from the company's "Security Department" will arrive. If, after interviewing you, he thinks you're serious and not just paranoid, he'll check your connections out, from the phone itself to the pole outside, and from the central exchange as well. This is a free service. ("After all, it's our phone and our wires," said one service representative.)

Some people can't bear to say good-bye

The longest telephone connection on record was one of 550 hours, lasting from November 28 to December 21, 1966, between co-eds on the seventh floors of Moore and Ford Halls at Kansas State University in Manhattan, Kansas.

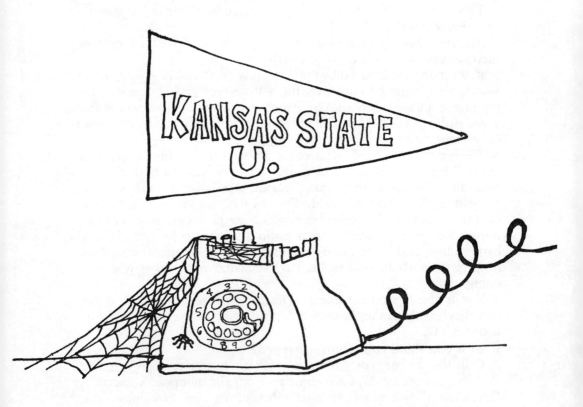

One day you look at the phone bill and you realize your child is a teen-ager.

A TELEPHONE MIRACLE

You can phone your friend in his home or office, have him pick a card from a deck, and, sitting by the phone in your own home or office, tell him which card he picked.

Here's how you do it. After your friend has picked his card (or just thought of it), have him double the numerical value (the value of a Jack is 11, a Queen is 12, and a King is 13). After doubling the value, ask him to add one and multiply the total by five.

If his card is a Club he should next add six to this total; if a Heart, he should add seven; if a Spade, he should add eight; and if a Diamond, he should add nine. Now ask him for the total and, with a little calculation, you can tell him the card.

The last digit of his total will always be either one, two, three, or four. If it's one, his suit is Clubs; if it's two, the suit is Hearts; if it's three, the suit is Spades; if it's four, the suit is Diamonds.

You can tell the number of his card by subtracting one from the number or numbers preceding the last digit in his announced total. For example, if his total is 74, the four indicates that his card is a Diamond. Subtract one from the seven and you know his card is six.

Here's an example of how it works: Let's say your friend chose the Jack of Clubs. The numeric value of the card is 11. He doubles it to 22. Then he adds one, making 23. Now he multiplies by five to equal 115. Then he adds six for Clubs, getting 121, and tells you that number. The last digit (one) tells you the suit is Clubs. Subtract one from the remaining digits (12), and you get 11, which represents the Jack.

The telephone chord

Not too long ago people were able to tune their musical instruments by listening to the dial tone (a nice, soft B-flat), but then Bell changed the tone to a "chord," two different frequencies carefully selected so that they wouldn't confuse Bell's internal equipment, programmed for push-button calling. The tones selected for the new dial signal were put into use only after it was determined that the computers wouldn't be fouled up by television noises and music on the radio.

The Motown sound

When the Bell System introduced push-button phone service a few years ago, it could hardly have anticipated that the push-button phone would become America's most popular new musical instrument.

Each of its buttons produces a different musical tone. If you punch out 33363213, you'll get a respectable rendition of "Raindrops Keep Fallin' on My Head"; 0005 8883 plays the first bars of Beethoven's *Fifth Symphony*; and 1199009 gives you "Twinkle, Twinkle, Little Star." It's unwise to try it, however, unless you call a friend first for the recital, or punch out your tunes over the time service recording, because otherwise you might find yourself inadvertently serenading someone expensively by long distance.

Push-button phone playing supposedly began in Detroit, where a pre-med student at Eastern Michigan University, Kenneth Ascher, called a WXYZ disc jockey and said, "Hey, listen to this." Telephone tunesmiths now are even learning how to get staccato and legato on appropriate notes, and the fad has produced at least two songbooks for the cult.

The phone company sees the craze as a potential problem. "We really think a phone is for communcation," said a Michigan Bell man, "not a replacement for the piano or violin."

* * *

Son: I'm broke and I need a hundred bucks right away.
Father: There must be something wrong with the line...I can't hear you.
Son: I say I want to borrow one hundred dollars.
Father: Boy, I can't hear a word you're saying.
(Operator cuts in) Hello, this is the operator...I can hear him very plainly.
Father: Then you lend him the hundred dollars!

Dates to remember
(while waiting for the phone to ring)

June 3, 1875: The first telephone constructed and human sounds heard. Boston.

March 10, 1876: The first complete sentences clearly understood over a telephone. Boston.

July 7-12, 1876: The first attempts to transmit speech over telegraph wires. Boston.

August, 1876: The first successful attempt to transmit speech over telegraph wires. Brantford, Ontario.

August, 1876: The first public demonstration of transmitting speech over telegraph lines. Brantford.

August, 1876: The first transmission of a number of voices over telegraph lines. Brantford. (The line used was eight miles long, from Brantford to nearby Paris, Ontario.)

October 9, 1876: The first conversation (reciprocal communication) over a telegraph line. Boston.

December 3, 1876: The first long-distance call over a telegraph line (143 miles). From Boston.

February 13, 1877: The first newspaper dispatch sent by telephone. Salem, Mass.

April 4, 1877: The first telephone line opened. Boston.

Wired for sound—The Bell System uses some 700 million miles of wire circuitry—more than enough to string a direct line to Jupiter, or to Mars and back three times.

PHONE EXERCISES

Before you dial:

The phone itself can be used like a piece of gym equipment. Take one end of the receiver in each hand and try to push the ends together. Then try to pull them apart. Start out gently the first day, holding for a count of two or three. Gradually add a little more strength each day you do the exercise, working your way up to a count of five or six. Do it often before dialing your call. This exercise strengthens your hands and chest muscles, as well as relieving tension. It does not weaken the phone.

While you're on hold:

Learning the art of proper breathing is an important factor in tension control. First relax and "think calm." Inhale to the count of three. As you exhale, follow with your mind the movement of your breath through your body. Now relax for a count of three. This exercise, called "basic breathing," gives you something productive to do while you're being held captive by that red button.

When the phone rings:

Stand up to answer without using the arms of your chair for assistance. Depending, of course, on how many calls you get, this can vastly strengthen stomach muscles—and if it's the Army Chief of Staff calling, you'll already be at attention.

Going, going . . . down

Long-distance calling keeps getting cheaper over the years. Back in 1928, cross-country calls cost $9 to make. Now, if you dial direct, the maximum charge is $1.35 for three minutes (70¢ on weekends.)

WORD SQUARES

The point of this game is to form words out of letters called out alternately by you and your phone friend. Here's how you play:

First draw a square and divide it into 25 boxes. The player who goes first now calls out a letter that both he and the person at the other end of the line place anywhere they wish in the boxes in front of them. The second player now calls out a letter and once more both players put the letter anywhere in the boxes they wish. In this way, alternating the calls, the 25 boxes are filled up with 25 letters.

Each player attempts to form as many words as he can out of those 25 letters, working horizontally or vertically. A five-letter word is five points, a four-letter word is four points, etc. Thus, if a player is able to form the word "TRAIN," he can get five points for "TRAIN," four points for "RAIN," and two points for "IN."

The key is thinking ahead not only about the words you wish to make from the letters you call yourself, but about the words you can make using the letters called out by your phone friend.

The game can be made more difficult by increasing the number of boxes and by allowing the players to form words not only vertically and horizontally, but also diagonally.

What's WATS?

Businesses that make a great many long-distance calls have found it profitable to install WATS lines. A WATS line ("Wide Area Telephone Service") allows them an unlimited number of long-distance calls for a fixed monthly rate or the option of purchasing ten hours of usage a month with additional time charged by the hour.

There are two types of WATS lines: interstate and intrastate. The interstate WATS service excludes the home state. AT&T has divided the nation into six service areas; WATS users can lease service for any number of areas they desire, with rates based on the number of areas included. Rates for intrastate WATS lines vary from state to state.

The long and short of it

Have you ever wondered why calls across vast distances often cost very little, while frequently called numbers just a few miles away put tolls on your bill? The phone company explains it this way: "So much of the basic cost is the switching apparatus at each end in setting up the connection—with or without the operator—and in billing the call. The distance over which the call goes is not so important once the hookup is made. For example, the charge for a night call is the same whether you're talking across 2,000 miles or 3,000 miles."

For whom Bell's toll's free

There are approximately 12,000 numbers in the United States that you can call long-distance without charge. To determine if a company has a toll-free line, call (800) 555-1212.

Mon Dieu!

On the average, a U.S. worker puts in about two hours' work to pay for his monthly telephone service. In London, for comparable service, workers have to chalk up four and a half hours' labor. In Brussels, it's about eight hours, and the poor Parisian has to work a full 15 hours to pay for his phone every month.

NUMBER DOODLES

Turn telephone numbers into brilliant doodles! That's not a promise, that's an order! Get started now or I'll come over to your house and beat up on the mice in your walls.

balancing bagels.

VINO

Persian caterwauling

The telephone made its debut in Iran before 1935 (when the country was still known as Persia) in a somewhat inauspicious fashion. The trouble began when the new Shah, with a startling display of innocence and over-confidence, had the country's first telephone line installed between his palace and the public market-place in Teheran. He then invited his subjects to call him up whenever they had grievances. Unfortunately, they took him up on his offer—by the hundreds daily, and their calls were so laced with abuse and obscenities that the Shah felt compelled to send his soldiers out to put down the apparent rebellion. When the soldiers fired on the parliament buildings, a real rebellion started, and the Shah had to flee the country.

PHONE GAME: CATEGORIES

You and your telephone friend should choose any mutually agreeable five-letter word (preferably one without duplicate letters), and each place it at the top of a page with the letters well spaced out.

Along the left-hand side of your page, each one making an alternate suggestion, you then write categories of any kind. For example: Sports, Writers, Movies, Cars, Foods, Political Leaders, Television Stars, etc.

The object of the game is to find something in each category (name of a sport, writer, political leader, etc.) that begins with the letters at the top of the column.

For example: If you used the word "PHONE" at the top of the page, the partially completed page might look like this:

	P	H	O	N	E
CAR	Pontiac	Hudson	Olds	Nash	Edsel
SPORT		Hockey			
FOOD	Peas	Hominy	Onions		Eggs
TV STAR	E			Gary Owens	
MOVIE		Harrad Experiment			

After you and your friend have decided on the categories, hang up. The first one to call back with a completed page wins.

The first 16 are out of order

The busiest pay phone in the world is in booth 17 in Manhattan's Grand Central Terminal. It handles more than 50,000 calls a year, during which time its users wear out (or rip out) at least 100 directories.

East side, west side, all around the town

New York City's pay phones are the most susceptible to damage by vandals, thieves, and pranksters. At least 25% of Manhattan's sidewalk phones are out of order at any given time. Out of more than 100,000 pay phones, an average of 35,000 are replaced or repaired annually. The most frequent damage comes from the picking of coin box locks. One thief reported hitting between 20 and 30 booths a day, from which he netted upwards of $20,000 a year.

The battered booth syndrome

Pay phones have been called "Ma Bell's Migraine," and not without reason. Every year they are kicked, bashed, or pulled apart by vandals, thieves, and disgruntled users. It costs the Bell System $3 million a year in stolen coins and $10 million in repairs and replacements. These losses, however, amount to less than one-tenth of one percent of AT&T revenues.

Test your eyesight: look up a number

That small print you find in your phone book was specially designed for the Bell System. It's called "Bell Gothic" and is used by opticians to test for sight problems. At one time, Bell considered supplying special magnifying glasses with each directory, but the company decided that they would probably be lost by home subscribers and stolen from telephone booths.

The Manhattan 25

Packed into the columns of the phone directory of any large city is a wealth of information other than phone numbers. A recent Manhattan directory, for example, contained in its 800,000 entries not only an index to the ethnic composition of the city, but also some interesting footnotes to the history of immigration to the United States. The most frequently listed surnames, in order, were:

1. Smith	14. Levine
2. Brown	15. Levy
3. Johnson	16. Wilson
4. Williams	17. Lewis
5. Cohen	18. Rodriguez
6. Miller	19. Friedman
7. Jones	20. Taylor
8. Schwartz	21. Clark
9. Davis	22. Robinson
10. Green	23. Klein
11. White	24. Jackson
12. Harris	25. Martin
13. Lee	

Six of the names are German or Jewish in origin and one is Spanish; the remainder are English or Welsh. Oddly enough, there are no Irish names on the list. Of the 18 English and Welsh names, all appear also in the top 30 of the London directory, and 15 of them are in London's top 20 (in approximately the same order.)

1. ~~SMITH~~ O'HARA
2. BROWN
3. JOHNSON
4. WILLIAMS
5. COHEN
6. MILLER
7. JONES
8. SCHWARTZ
9. DAVIS
10. GREEN
11. WHITE
12. HARRIS
13. LEE
14. LEVINE
15. LEVY
16. WILSON

Employing retired telephone directories

Used telephone books have been put to some unusual uses. Errol Garner, the jazz pianist, puts one on his bench when he plays. A South American banana company bought 800 to pad the walls of its freight cars and payroll trucks to keep bandits from shooting them up. Secret agents have been known to use the directory as a coding device, basing their alphabetical key on the first and last listings on a given page. In the sixties a woman was jailed in West Germany for selling stolen Manhattan directories to Communist agents for $75 each. (She must have been quite a saleswoman, considering that any non-subscriber can buy the directories from New York Telephone for about $3 each.)

The Library of Congress keeps back issues of directories as well as current ones, of which they have about 1,800. They have more than 26,000 out-of-date directories.

Literacy tests for subscribers

Pity the poor bureaucrats who were responsible for inventing exchange names. Apart from spelling and phonetics, they had to consider subscriber psychology as well. In New York, Byfleet was considered for a time, but it was dropped because the phone company knew it would be too often dialed BIfleet. Subscribers wanting the CYpress exchange often dialed CIpress and even SIpress instead. BOulevard became BUlevard, and so on. Hundreds of callers unfamiliar with Pennsylvania Dutch stumbled over EPhrata. In Philadelphia, there was a CYnwyd exchange (pronounced Kinwid), which was often dialed KI. VIrginia proved a poor exchange name, for callers, tending to visualize it in terms of its abbreviation, dialed VA. Even New York's venerable MUrray Hill sometimes came out MH.

Bell's letters

The better to understand you with, phone company operators use the following alphabet code:

A as in Alice	N as in Nellie
B as in Bertha	O as in Oliver
C as in Charles	P as in Peter
D as in David	Q as in Quaker
E as in Edward	R as in Robert
F as in Frank	S as in Samuel
G as in George	T as in Thomas
H as in Harry	U as in Utah
I as in Ida	V as in Victor
J as in James	W as in William
K as in Kate	X as in X ray
L as in Louis	Y as in Young
M as in Mary	Z as in Zebra

Topless Librarians
Forklifts
No Batteries Needed
Noiseless
Have Your Fork Be Instantly
Six Inches Taller

CRIMINAL BUREAU INC
*Analyzing Suspicious Stains -
Handwriting
Surveillance And Personal Protection
Devices*
08Hector   Conshohocken------232-4

MERKINS
ADULT BOOK STORE
AND CHURCH

72-355
1 E AIRY - NORRISTOWN

A' DORO-BOB
   428E Hennessy Rd H-727971
A E C (H K) LTD
   Chartered Bk Bldg ..H-246408
   97 Caine Rd H-242485
A E & Co, Wing On Central Bldg ..H-235281
   Do H-230412
A E Wigs Wing On Central Bldg ..H-235281
A FAT & CO
   P & O Bldg H-232853
   Do H-231613
A Go Go Bar 61 Hennessy Rd H-732548
A Jim & Co Harold Jim
   Res Fontana Bldg H-771352

A Chack, 68 Hennessy Rd H-733330
A Ching, 38 Pottinger St H-237837

A Kau Sailmaker, 180 Gloucester Rd H-744795
A King Slipway, 78 Electric Rd ..H-705326
   IL 6675 Hing Fat St H-704469
   Do H-704468
   Do H-704677
   101 Electric Rd H-704639
   Ah Kung Ngam H-601502
   78 Electric Rd H-719514
A Koodhus, Wang Kee Bldg H-235961
A Kwai & Co 95 Lockhart Rd H-732721
   Do H-736910
A Lam Sail Maker
   229 Shaukiwan Rd H-603476
A LAM WATCH CO
   Man Yee Bldg H-236803

If It's in Our Yellow Pages & You
Can't Get There in Person—Then You
Know It's **Phoney**

Cor Ralph&Williams Dntn

MAMA & POPPA
WHEELY'S
MOTORCYCLE
PLACE
25-7159
NEAR LAKEWOOD BLVD.

CONFIDENTIAL FREE CONSULTATION
A PHONE CALL BRINGS AN AGENT
UNDERCOVER, SURVEILLANCE
"PICTURES TELL THE STORY"

Estates Appraised & Purchased
A Lau 14 Pedder St H-242792

CALL TU 4-112   **9**

BLOCK DISTRIBUTORS
107 WGlenwoodAv Phila-   -MO 7-183

ALL NIGHT SHOE REPAIR STAND
418 Newton 749-704

A good question

James Thurber had the perfect answer for people who told him he had reached the wrong number: "If this is the wrong number, why did you answer the phone?"

Thurber, who considered telephones among his natural enemies, told the story of the opening night on Broadway of a particularly boring play, whose third-act curtain went up on an empty stage and a ringing phone. The phone rang and rang and rang. Apparently the actor responsible for answering it had missed his cue. Robert Benchley, who had been dozing in his seat through the first two acts, was suddenly aroused by the insistent ringing and shouted out, "Why doesn't somebody answer that? I think it's for me." The next day one of the critics said, "The only amusing line in the play was spoken by Bob Benchley who, unhappily, was not in the cast."

AN EVEN-MORE-ODD CARD TRICK

Here's an exceedingly simple card trick. Using it, you can predict how many cards a phone friend has in his hand and, when he divides them into two piles, which pile will contain an odd number of cards and which an even number.

Have your friend take any two-digit number. Tell him to add the digits of this number, subtract this amount from the original number (e.g., 41 - 5 = 36), and then add the digits of that answer—the result will always be 9. For example: the two digit number is 41; add the digits (4 + 1 = 5); subtract five from 41 (41 - 5 = 36); add the digits (3 + 6 = 9). It will always come out to nine and this fact is the basis of the trick.

This formula can be used as the basis for a card trick in the following way:

Have the person on the other end of the phone take any number of cards more than ten from the deck. If he takes 12, the digits (1 + 2) add up to three. Subtract three from the original number (12) and put them aside. Now he has nine cards in his hand, as you well know, but he doesn't know that you know.

Now tell him that, although you don't know the number of cards he has, you can predict that, if he lays down the cards in two piles, one will have an odd number and the other will have an even number, and that you can tell him which is which. Tell him to start laying out the cards, first one on the left, then one on the right alternately. The right will always have an even number (4) and the left an odd number (5).

One of history's less successful advertising campaigns

For many years, the Bell System did its best to discourage the use of "Hello" in answering the phone. In the forties it even launched an advertising campaign aimed at getting rid of the dreaded word. Subscribers received blotters inscribed with the following message, entitled "Who is 'Hello'?"

> Hello means very little over the telephone. It gives no information except that someone has answered. A grunt, while not so polite, would serve the same purpose.

> Think of the time that would be saved if all telephones were answered: *Mr. Smith*, or simply, *Smith*. Or in the case of departmental telephones, *Treasurer's Office, Miss Jones*.

> Answers like this give all necessary information in a nut-shell, save time, and help clear your line for other important calls.

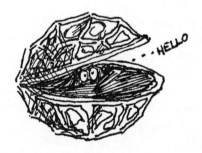

Hello, good-bye

For those who like to call long, long distance, here are 16 ways in which you can begin and end your conversation:

	Hello	Good-bye
German	hallo	auf Wiedersehen
Dutch	hallo	goeie dag
Swedish	hallà	adjö
Norwegian	hallo	farvel
Danish	hallo	farvel
French	allò	bonjour/baï baï
Italian	pronto	arrivederci/ciao
Spanish	diga	adiós
Portuguese	pega	adeus
Armenian	ayo	mnas parov
Polish	hallo	zegnam
Czech	ano	bohem
Turkish	alo	allaha ismarla
Japanese	moshi	sayonara
Malayan	hai	jalan
Hawaiian	aloha	aloha

* * *

The nationality of telephone girls in the early 1900s was Central American.

TAT tales

The first transatlantic call was made in 1915 by radiotelephone. H. R. Shreeve, stationed at the Eiffel Tower in Paris, heard the words " . . . and now, Shreeve, good night" addressed to him by B. B. Webb. In its first year of operation, the London-New York radiotelephone circuit handled 2,300 calls. Radiotelephony, however, had its limitations. The number of bands, or frequencies, was limited and there was much competition for the use of these frequencies by aviation and marine broadcasting, and by other concerns.

Obviously, a submarine telephone cable was needed, but such a communication line had to wait until undersea amplifiers, or repeaters, could be developed—and these did not come along until 1950, when they were put into service between Key West and Havana. The first transatlantic cable, TAT-1, was laid out in 1956 between Clarenville, Newfoundland, and Oban, Scotland, a distance of 2,240 statute miles. American and British companies manufactured the cable.

Three years later, TAT-2 was laid between Penmarch, France, and Clarenville, to be shared by Bell and the French and West German telephone organizations. French, German, and American companies manufactured the equipment, and five European countries bought permanent rights to use its circuits.

The first two TAT's were twin-cable systems, with one line for each direction of speech. Repeaters were placed at 40-mile intervals and the cables provided only 48 circuits for use only up to 2,650 miles. Similar cables were laid from the lower states to Alaska, to Hawaii, and to Puerto Rico, but they were deemed obsolete the day they were opened, and Bell engineers quickly designed single two-way cables with 128 circuits each and a range of 4,000 miles. To do this, the repeaters had to be spaced every 20 miles.

Modern repeaters take more than a year to build and test, and are designed to last 20 years without malfunction in any of their 5,000 precision parts. Each tiny vacuum tube alone costs more than a Volkswagen. The tests they're put through are so rigorous that the sealed cylindrical housing cannot leak more than a thimbleful in 25 years.

Ah so, y'all

Telephone service on the first cable between the United States and Japan was inaugurated on June 18, 1964, with a call from President Johnson to Premier Ikeda. The cable, stretching 5,300 nautical miles from Oahu, Hawaii to Japan, via Midway, Wake, and Guam, joined existing cables from Hawaii to the U.S. mainland. Its capacity was 138 voice channels; its cost, $80 million.

MORE PENCIL STUNTS

The next time Aunt Edna calls to describe (a) her retirement party, (b) her raft trip down the Colorado River, (c) her leg transplant, or (d) the mysterious disappearance of Uncle Harry—don't hang up. Just make some agreeable noises and try the following puzzles—first with your finger and then with your pencil.

Trace the one on the left and at the bottom in one continuous line without crossing any lines or lifting your pencil. For the one on the right, see if you can *cross* all the lines between the dots in one continuous line without crossing or retracing your line. Solutions are on page 117.

What communication gap?

Have you ever noticed that it's often easier to talk over the phone about certain things that you couldn't say to a person in his presence? A California woman who had trouble talking to her family because she couldn't compete with TV, books, magazines, and newspapers, tried calling them from the kitchen extension. Before asking to speak to the boy's father, she learned all sorts of things about her 14-year-old son—what he'd been doing in school, what sports he was going out for, etc. She asked him, too, why he had so much to say on the phone. "It's easy," he said, "when you don't have to look at people."

High telephone density

Although the United States has about 45% of the world's telephones, it ranks only second in phones per capita. First is Monaco, with 54 phones for every 100 citizens. The royal palace alone has more than 100 phones, which helps keep the average up in a principality with only 23,000 people.

Low telephone density

The Himalayan republic of Bhutan ranks last in number of phones per capita. It has no phones at all.

Fastest phones in the East

There are more than five million telephones for New Jersey's seven million residents, and it seems they stay in fairly constant use. In its 1973 annual report, New Jersey Bell announced that the state's average subscriber made 1,100 calls in the previous year, the highest average in the world, and 270 calls above the national average.

Wouldn't you know it?

The biggest private line user in the entire Bell System is the U.S. government. It operates a private voice and data network to interconnect the 750,000 telephones of its civil agencies throughout the country.

Peak traffic

One of the highest telephones in the world is located atop Mount Rosa in the Italian Alps. It was installed by Queen Margherita of Italy so that she could converse daily with her favorite astronomer, Professor Mosso, who studied the stars from an observatory on the peak. It took a crew of laborers six years to get the telephone lines up the mountain.

No wonder they get into so much mischief

The largest single telephone network in the world is in the Pentagon. There are 50,000 telephones in the building, and the Pentagon's switchboard handles an average of 270,000 calls each day.

PENTAGON TELEPHONE PUZZLE MAZE

Of the 270,000 calls per day mentioned above, 200,000 are from people calling to guess where General Kreeblemeyer has left his cufflink. The winner gets an all-expense trip via tank to Fort Campbell, Kentucky, near Paducah. Now, with your pencil in hand, see if you can find the missing link.

TELEPHONE NUMBER PERCEPTION

With this trick you ask your telephone friend to cross out any number in a telephone number, and you are able to tell him the exact number he crossed out.

First, ask the person on the other end of the phone to write down any telephone number. Then have him add together all the digits, and subtract the total of that addition from the original number. For example, if he starts off with the number 828-8755, the total of the digits is 43, and 43 subtracted from 828-8755 is 828-8712.

Next have him take this number (828-8712) and cross out any digit, and then give you the total of the remaining digits. For example, if he crossed out the 7, the total of the remaining digits would be 29 $(8 + 2 + 8 + 8 + 1 + 2 = 29)$.

You can now tell him what number he has crossed out by performing a very simple calculation. Subtract the number that your friend arrived at by this last calculation (29) from the nearest multiple of 9 that is a higher number. In this case, it would be 36; 29 from 36 equals 7, the very number that your friend crossed out.

Here is another example. Initial number: 321-4506. Total of the digits is 21. Subtract 21 from 321-4506. The result is 321-4485. Now cross out one digit, let's say the 8. Add the remaining digits, $3 + 2 + 1 + 4 + 4 + 5 = 19$. Subtract 19 from the nearest higher multiple of 9, which would be 27. 27 minus 19 equals 8, the number crossed out.

If the total of the final calculation adds up to a multiple of 9, e.g., 9, 18, 27, 36, 45, then the number that your friend has crossed out is either a 9 or 0. You can get him to reveal which one by asking the question, "Is it a round number?" If he says yes, it's the zero. If he says no, it must be the 9.

Metropolitan millionaires

In January, 1972, 19 cities in the world had more than one million telephones. They were:

New York	5,825,460
Tokyo	4,959,707
Los Angeles	4,942,510
London	3,782,828
Paris	2,797,840
Osaka	2,685,109
Chicago	2,358,668
Moscow	1,625,000
Philadelphia	1,545,192
Detroit	1,384,820
Minneapolis-St.Paul	1,306,300
Rome	1,168,672
Buenos Aires	1,115,304
Madrid	1,106,676
Baltimore	1,104,806
Sydney	1,101,618
Montreal	1,030,481
Houston	1,009,193
Milan	1,006,796

*   *   *

Phone company: So I understand that you refuse to pay for the 200 long-distance calls we have charged against you.
Customer: Exactly!
Phone company: But what is your reason?
Customer: I don't have a telephone.

Solutions for puzzle on page 33:

1. 2   6. 2
2. 6   7. 5
3. 4   8. 0
4. 3   9. 1
5. 0   10. 13

Solutions for puzzles on page 66:

Solutions for puzzles on page 110:

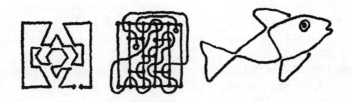

Getting the right number

Patent No. 174,465 was issued on March 7, 1876, to Alexander Graham Bell for his telephone. It has been called "the most valuable single patent ever issued." Probably no one would contest that, and for that reason the patent itself was hotly contested. In the next 11 years after it was issued, Bell had to fight 600 separate lawsuits challenging his rights. The most persistent litigant was a Chicagoan named Elisha Gray, who went to his grave insisting that he was the true inventor.

The Gray Telephone Hour?

And on the seventh day he rested

After inventing the telephone, Alexander Graham Bell didn't rest on his laurels. Not only did he make several improvements to the telephone, but he also went on to invent the aileron, an X-ray device, the action comic strip, a system of air conditioning, an echo device similar to today's sonar, an electrical probe for surgeons, the wax-disc phonograph record, an iron lung, a method for using radium in cancer treatment, a sound detector for locating icebergs, and a device to take husks from wheat before grinding. He also devised a method for changing sea water into drinking water, thought up the idea of lasers, and developed two new breeds of sheep.

Wall Telephone c. 1913